Rats, Mice, And Other Things You Can't Take to The Bank

An Inspirational Collection of Essays from Humorous to Simply Human

By Leslie Handler

Cover Design by Dwayne Booth

Published 2018 by HumorOutcasts Press
Printed in the United States of America

ISBN: 0-9994127-3-6
EAN-13: 978-0-9994127-3-2

Dedicated to Marty, who knew I had an itch and let me scratch it.

Table of Contents

Prologue

Taken from the book *Oh, Rats!: The Story of Rats and People:*

"Everything about the rat makes it a champion at survival. Of all the mammals, only humans have been more successful—at least so far. Just think about what a rat can do. It can:

· squeeze through a pipe the width of a quarter

· scale a brick wall, straight up

· fall off a five-story building and land safely on its feet

· rear up on its hind legs and box with its front paws

· get flushed down a toilet and live

· climb up a drainpipe into a toilet bowl"

In El Puig, Spain there is a fiesta every year on the last Sunday in January. Aside from the traditional food and dance, they celebrate the holiday with the custom of the throwing of the rats. Perhaps they do this to cleanse their homes in preparation for a new year. Whatever the reason, the rats survive, and find their way back into people's homes year after year.

One Manhattan exterminator was once quoted as saying that rats surviving to age 4 grow exponentially wiser. "A trap means nothing to them, no matter how skillfully set," the exterminator says. "They just kick it around until it snaps; then they eat the bait. I believe some of them can even read."

Even in modern day technology, RAT is an acronym, short for Remote Access Trojan, a Trojan horse that provides the intruder, or hacker, with a backdoor into the infected system. This backdoor allows the hacker to snoop your system, use your infected system to launch a zombie (attacks on other systems), or even run malicious code.

Rats may be used in sentences as synonyms for betrayers, scoundrels, and spreaders of disease, but they are mammals, just like us. Webster's dictionary defines "oh rats" as the exclamation used to express mild annoyance or irritation.

But without question, whether you use the word "rats" in place of the word "damn," whether you scream at the sight of them, or try to do the trap and toss, it cannot be denied, that they can always find a backdoor, they become wiser over time, and they are above all, survivors. As for me, well I'm a survivor too!

Introduction

I was born. I thought this would be a fascinating way to start this essay collection. It's so unique. You never would have known it. I almost started that first line with "Call me Ishmael," but it's been taken. My life's been full of so many ups and downs, that I thought perhaps I'd start with "It was the best of times. It was the worst of times." But I heard that one was taken too.

So yea, I was born. I'd tell you all about the trip, you know, the journey down the birth canal, etc, but in all honesty, I just can't remember it. You see, I'm old now, and I don't remember much.

There it is. I was born, and now I'm old. The end.

Ok, I'll admit it. There's been a whole lot of stuff in between. I'd like to say that I've lived my life as a glass half full kind of person, but that wouldn't be entirely true. Yet, without a doubt, I have not lived my life as a glass half empty person either. What I can say is that I've had my fill of empty glasses. I let them get empty. I think that sometimes I have found myself in circumstances in which I had no choice for the contents in them to evaporate. Sometimes, I have had a choice, and I've allowed the glass to empty completely anyway. And you know what? For me, that's been ok. Because once that glass is empty, there's just nowhere else to go but to fill it back up. Sometimes I fill it slowly. Sometimes I fill it with gusto as quickly as a brand-new sports car accelerating on the open road with no cops around. But one way or another, that glass always gets filled right back up. So I guess you could say that I'm like most everyone else in the world. I've been dealt my share of crap. But unlike some, I'm actually grateful for my crap. I'm grateful because when it ends, and it always ends, I fill my glass right back up. When it's full again, I'm grateful and more appreciative because I remember how it felt when it was empty. And when I'm lucky...when I'm very, very lucky, sometimes, it even overflows. And those, those are the glasses you hold on to for as long as you can, because those are the ones that make life itself worth living. I've had the ultimate fortune in having a whole lot of those.

Please come join me in my journey. No matter where you find yourself in life right now, I hope that my words will add a few more drops to your glass until you find the rim overflowing for you as well.

<u>Chapter One: Dates, Dogs, and Even Rats</u>

Games, games, games

The boys I dated were mostly affluent. In high school I had a double date with one of Ross Perot's daughters, Nancy. Actually, it was a triple date. The three girls were to meet at my house to make a picnic dinner. The guys were to pick us up to take us to Shakespeare in the park. Nancy showed up two hours late. We had already made the fried chicken and the dessert, all that was left was the potato salad when Nancy arrived. The boys were to be there in forty-five minutes, so my other girlfriend and I left my mom in the kitchen with Nancy while we went upstairs to spruce up. Mom showed Nancy the bowl of potatoes and other ingredients and gave her a pot and other necessary utensils and told her she'd be back in a few minutes. By the time my mom returned, Nancy had cut up a bowl full of raw potatoes filled with mayo and spices. So much for rich girls knowing how to cook. But then again, I'm not sure why I expected anything less since the first time I met her she asked to borrow a quarter for the cafeteria soda machine. She never did pay that quarter back.

As for the boys, they picked us up on time, we had a lovely picnic, sans potato salad, and I don't recall really ever interacting much with Nancy for the rest of high school. She was a lovely girl. I guess you could just say we ran in different crowds.

I had lots of exciting dates in those years. At the time, I wanted to pursue going into the hotel business, so I got myself a job at the finest hotel in town and spent a summer getting to know everyone from the housekeeping staff to the head maître 'd of the finest restaurant there, to the general manager. One of my dates, decided he would impress me by taking me to dinner there. Apparently, he dined there often and thought he'd impress me when the waiters all knew him by name, but by the time he was taken to our table, he found himself alone. When he turned to see where I was, he found me hugging and kissing all the wait staff and calling them all by their first names. After I watched my date pick his jaw up off the floor, we managed to have a lovely evening with no need to further attempt to impress one another. I dated this boy on and off for several years before I met my husband. He was fun, and treated me well, but I never did feel much substance there. He used to pick me up in a different car every time we went out. There was the Trans Am, the Mercedes, and the Porsche to name a few. My mom said that when he picked me up in the Rolls Royce, that would just have to be the last date because as she put it, "where do you go from there?" You know? She was right. That was our last date.

But I had other great dates with lots of other guys throughout high school and college. My favorite dates though, were dates with my dad. He always wanted to have special time with me. I'd get all dressed up and we'd go out on the town. Sometimes he'd take me to a show, sometimes to lunch, sometimes even to dinner. But going out with Dad always meant special time and to this day brings cherished memories.

Mom was the softy. Dad was the disciplinarian. Both gave me and my older brother nothing but love and support for our entire lives.

In this first chapter, I tell you all about these stories and even more stories about my growing up. Like so many children, one of the things I begged for was a family pet. At one point, my folks went out and bought a boxer puppy....this from two people who knew nothing about raising a small animal let alone a boxer. They blinked and "Happy" the dog, became an untrained, crazed, lunatic beast who hung himself by his own chain over the back yard fence. The good news is that Happy lived to tell the tale, and kept his tail as well. The next day, I was told he ran away. Years later Dad tried a Mynah bird. Between the screeching and the feces throwing, that one didn't work out too well either. Eventually, I received an untrained Bichon Frise of unknown age who became one of the loves of my life and the bane of my mother's existence. His name was Pierre, but mom called him the carpenter dog because he did odd jobs around the house: a little pee here, a little food dumping there. But for me, from then on, I was a dog lover.

You'll hear more stories about my animal adventures throughout my life. You'll also hear about one of my family's earliest challenges regarding my loving brother and my first lessons in hate, love, and the power they each have.

Finally, I leave you with this early memory. It's one of my favorites and it explains why rats have been in my life.

I could smell the chlorine filling my nostrils as I quenched my thirst from the water flowing from the garden hose. I could see those waves of heat floating in the Texas air on a hundred-degree summer's day. We'd hook the sprinkler up to the hose and run bare foot through the water and the soft iridescent grass that could never be too green in the southwestern sultriness. When we were finally cool enough, we'd wrap ourselves in the thickness of terrycloth towels, dry off, and head inside for a read-a-thon in the air conditioned coolness of our home.

In the winter months, there was nothing more enticing than a pile of pillows and blankets placed before a roaring wood-burning fire. But even the smell of the smoke escaping up the chimney with the remnants of roasted marshmallows trailing its sugary aroma wasn't as good as what was to come. The best part, was the sweet smell of the drying hair of my two little girls fresh from the tub-all squeaky clean with the scent of youth. I can remember the little hairs inside my nose would vibrate and tickle when we would crack open that first book of the day. I would suck up those freshly printed pages with a deep inhale offering up that first book to the noses of my girls. They too could sniff the words right off their pages and into their hearts. The flicker of the fire light would illuminate the beautiful faces of my girls as we began the first adventure of the day into the world of books. At their youngest, there was Chick-a-Chick-a-Boom-Boom, Are You My Mother?, and any Berenstain Bears books. As they got older it became Goosebumps, Ella Enchanted, and eventually Harry Potter.

A Handler read-a-thon, whether in the heat of the summer, or the frigid days of winter, was our time, our special time, time to cherish each other away from the stresses of daily life. It was our escape, our escape together. In those days, aside from relieving ourselves of full bladders or empty tummies, there was only one thing that would get us to break away from our reading, and that, was a good board game.

One such board game was a game called "Oh Rats." Each player received his own puzzle. He had to take the puzzle apart and then take a turn spinning a board that showed one puzzle piece. If he didn't yet have that puzzle piece, he could use it to add towards the completion of his puzzle. If he already had it, he would shout out "oh rats," and it would be the next player's turn. The winner was the first person to complete his puzzle. I loved this game. I loved it because it taught the girls their shapes and colors, but I mostly loved it because it taught them about the frustrations in life of not always getting what you want, and being able to just chalk it up to an exclamation of "oh rats." To this day, when something doesn't quite go my way, I can just shout out "oh rats" and know that it's ok. There will always be another game, and there will always be more rats in the world. Finding the right balance and getting your puzzle all put together, well that makes all the difference.

With that, I hope you enjoy the following essays about my special family, how we think about dogs in our house, and if I left something out, "oh rats," I'll have to wait until my next book to explain it.

A Parade with History

Uncle Seymour was the Deputy Inspector of the New York City Police Department who led the raid on Stonewall on June 27, 1969. I'd like to say he was a bad man – a man who led the raid on the gay community. I'd like to say he was a good man - a man who did his job protecting the public by following the orders of his superiors. But it's not all that black and white. Uncle Seymour, like most of us, was somewhere in the middle. At the time, the New York City Police Department's excuse for raiding Stonewall was that it was run by the Mafia. They didn't mention the fact that such raids had become routine regardless of who ran the establishment. But there were two things that were different about this raid, on this day, led by this man. The first was that for the first time, the gay patrons rebelled. The second was that Uncle Seymour personally prevented any police weapons from being discharged, thus preventing an escalation of the rebellion and probable deaths.

Uncle Seymour was a WWII veteran, a husband, and a father. Uncle Seymour was also a Jew. Although he passed away almost four years ago, I'm sure if I'd had the opportunity to ask him, he would have told me that there was no excuse for Hitler's Nazis in Germany to exterminate Jews just because they were following orders. Amazingly, while he was still living, he admitted that had he had it to do over again, he still would have led the raid on Stonewall. It was his job. He was following the orders of his superiors. But he did admit to the prejudices of the police department at the time, and he was grateful that the incident shed light on the subject, opening the flood gates for future reform.

Two years after the Stonewall Riot, in 1971, I was eleven years old. My brother was thirteen. For a year or two, he had been allowed to stay at home alone with me to babysit when Mom and Dad went out. We actually relished a Saturday night at home without Mom and Dad. They'd be all dressed up to go out. Dad would have on a suit and tie; Mom would have on some glamorous sequined number. She would've spent half the day at the beauty parlor getting her hair done up in a beehive. I would've gone with her with my case of Barbies in tow playing at the foot of the salon stool while she gossiped and got beautified. They would've sprayed heavy lacquer hair spray all over the "do" before she left the salon. She would spray on more when she got home just for good measure. Then she would apply emerald green eye shadow from the lid of her eye to the line of her brow, glue on fake eyelashes, and roll on bright red lipstick before she walked out the door hand in hand with Dad after a good night kiss to each of us and a pat on the head.

Then the fun could begin. We'd run to the kitchen and turn on the oven, letting it preheat. Then to our separate bedrooms to put on our pjs. Back to the kitchen to put two TV dinners in. Then to the den to set up our TV tables and tune in to the Saturday night line-up of *The Mary Tyler Moore Show, Julia, and The Carol Burnett Show*. It was our little slice of heaven. We had always been close. He was my big brother and always took it upon himself to be my knight in shining armor. My parents tell of the time when I was two and he was four and he pushed a little boy who tried to steal my tricycle from me. From then on, he was my hero. He still is today.

But over time that all changed. My hero seemed to have gone on a sabbatical. That thirteen-year-old brother of mine, the one who played games with me and watched TV with me, was gone. In his place remained a teenage boy who had shut down. He became sullen and non-communicative. He made a beeline for his bedroom immediately after school every day. He only came out to eat dinner with us. Then he went right back into his room until we had to leave for school the next morning. To my recollection, this went on for close to five years. For two of those years, we went to high school together. At school I observed a gregarious brother, drum major of the band, lead in the school play, and award winner of science projects. At home I observed aloofness and a space alien who never came out of his habitat or removed the foreign object from covering his ears, the one you could hear music come out of in muffled tones.

Then one day the foreign being looked both ways before crossing the hallway to my side of the house. We were sixteen and eighteen then. He stated that we hadn't spent much time together lately and asked me if I wanted to go on a road trip with him. He apparently had planned this out for some time and had clearance from Mom and Dad. "What fun," I thought, "a road trip."

We had a pleasant enough drive and checked into a local hotel. His mood immediately shifted. He was nervous. He sat down on his bed and looked at me with a sternness I'd never seen in him before. He cleared his throat. I sat on my bed staring deep into his eyes afraid to say anything.

Something important was about to happen, but I just couldn't tell what. Then he said it. He said the two words that he had pent up inside him for an eternity. "I'm gay," he said.

I thought about this for all of three seconds before I responded. "OK," I said. And as far as I can recall at this oh-so-life-changing moment, that was that. I had never really thought about gays or about homosexuality at all. I didn't know any other homosexuals. At least I didn't know that I knew any other homosexuals. And I had never been taught anything about them. All I knew was that this was my brother. I loved him. This was important to him. It didn't make any difference to me. Now don't go giving me any credit here. I was by no means a forward thinker. I wasn't progressive. I was a flat-chested, pre-period, late bloomer who had no knowledge or opinion one way or another on the topic of sexuality. I did have knowledge, however, of my brother, and I had been missing him. We went about having a fun filled long weekend together and a renewed sibling relationship.

He went off to college the following fall. Over the years, he's filled in bits and pieces of information for me. It's painful for him. Those sullen years were his coming of age years. The years that are hard for all of us. But for him, a boy who felt different - a boy who was different - they were even harder. People didn't come out of the closet then. They hid in it. They hid in back alleys and seedy bars. There were no internet dating sites. There were no safe places to meet other people like him. There was no PFLAG. There were stories of shrinks, first sexual encounters, embarrassment, secrets, rejection, and shame.

I remember a time when he took me to hear a wonderful acapella group called "The Flirts". They were great. They did something at the beginning of their concert that made them forever emblazoned in my memory. They told stories: short one and two sentence stories about their lives without identifying which of them had experienced the story. One of them was kicked out of the house at the age of 12. One of them was beaten up repeatedly in school. One of them was gang raped. How many horrible stories did my brother experience?

It took time, but to my parent's amazing credit, they accepted him and loved him for who he was. They wanted to have a relationship with their son...their son who grew to become one of the most compassionate men I've ever known...their son who takes after them.

Mom, Dad, my brother, and I all grew up together learning to navigate the road of bigotry, ignorance, and hatred. We found ourselves in the nineties living independent lives that never strayed too far from the importance of family. I became a wife and a mother. My brother became the favorite uncle. Life was good until one chilly October day when I felt like an armadillo on the side of the road. First there was the jolt of the car hitting me. Then my guts splayed out onto the road - all bodily warmth evaporating into the cold fall air. I turned my face to my husband. It was a face filled with big fat tears, the ones that make your skin blotchy, your eyes puffy, and your saliva double in quantity. The ones that pinch up your face and collide with your snot; the ones that make you sound like a three-year-old gasping for breath as you try to explain yourself. I had just hung up from my brother. He was HIV positive. It was a death sentence.

All I could think of was that I was going to lose my brother again. But this time I would never be able to get him back. No one survived AIDS. Back then, I immediately made that leap. Everyone did. HIV, AIDS, there was no difference. It meant you were dying. He went out on disability. He sold his life insurance for the money. He started taking meds: a whole lot of meds with a whole lot of side effects. The next thing I knew, he also had Hepatitis C and started on a yearlong course of chemotherapy. Over time, new drugs were developed. He got his hands on the best of the best. To my great fortune my brother still lives today. He graces us with his warmth and generosity. He teaches us by example how to live a genuine life being true to who he is in spite of the bigotry, the hate, and the ignorance of the world.

San Francisco is where my brother now lives. He's lived there for over twenty years. He lives only a few blocks away from where the Pride Parade goes every year, every year since June 28th, 1970: the first anniversary of Stonewall. In all that time, he's only once attended the parade. He complains about it causing too much traffic, too much trash, and two much noise. But when I go to visit him, I see he keeps something special on his bookshelf. He keeps a collection of old tapes of *The Mary Tyler Moore Show*. It seems our pre-pubescent days were special to him too.

Finally, finally, he has met someone. A man who makes him happy. My family got to meet him this past Thanksgiving. We spent a lovely holiday together. We ate. We told stories. We exchanged gifts, and we laughed.

My own two girls are grown now. They each have special partners in their lives. I'll be hearing wedding bells soon for one of them. I hope to hear them for both my girls, and I hope to hear them for my brother because closets should be for clothes and shame and embarrassment for those who have done something wrong. My brother doesn't have to attend a pride parade every year if he doesn't want to because he has enough pride. He has the freedom to choose how he shows his pride. Uncle Seymour, in his own way, helped him have it.

A Lesson in Humility

When I was six years old I returned home from Sunday school with a wonderful new toy in hand. I don't think they make them anymore. It didn't have lights, or batteries, or a computer chip. It was a little plastic character with arms and legs. The appendages had tiny strings inside of them attached to a base. Under the base was a button that you could push to make the arms and legs move. It was a wondrous thing to behold when you're six. My father asked me where I got the toy, and I responded telling him that the teacher gave it to me. He proceeded to ask me if the teacher gave all the children in the class a toy. I told him that no, I was the only one who received a toy that day. He posed a rather obvious follow up question for me. He asked me why I received a toy and why none of the other children in class received one too. My answer surprised him. I told him that I received the toy because I was a special child. His questioning on this response went back and forth for some time before my father finally concluded that I was fibbing and that fibbing was punishable by a trip to my bedroom where upon arrival, I would be spending some length of time contemplating both my choice in room decor and my obviously damaged conscience.

One day, about this same time, I came home from public school, to proudly announce that I knew who Abraham Lincoln was. At the dinner table, I was asked to explain my knowledge of the man. With great confidence, I explained that he freed the Jewish slaves from Egypt. A roar of laughter circled the table at my expense. I was devastated at my family's reaction to my newfound knowledge.

After several weeks passed, we attended open house at Sunday school at which time my parents complimented me on my talent for drawing stick figure scenes of Egyptian Pharaohs, the bad guys, and my accomplishment on receiving a check plus on the answers I gave on a test about Moses, not Abraham Lincoln, who freed slaves, the Jewish kind, from Egypt.

On this very same expedition, my father found himself perusing the various posters on the walls of the classroom when I suddenly spotted him turning a brilliant shade of crimson. Even though I was only six, I can vividly recall the shade, the hue, and the tone of this particular shade of crimson and the particular manner in which he wore it. After I saw him having a brief conversation with the Sunday school teacher, he told us that it was time to go home. While I was getting ready for bed, dad knocked on my bedroom door and asked to have a talk with me. Now even at the tender age of six, I knew that when someone wants to have a talk with you, it can't be something good. So I made an enormous effort to zip my lip and open my ears. It was then that I found out why my father turned the brightest shade of red a man can turn. He told me that while at Sunday school, he saw the chart posted on the wall that listed the special child of the day. You see, each week, the teacher assigned one child to help pass out the papers and the crayons. That child, was the special child for the day and was rewarded at the end of the day, with a toy: a plastic push up toy to be exact.

My father came to me with humility in his eyes and an apology in his heart. I can recall being fairly forgiving, but forgetting, well that part never happened. Throughout the remainder of my childhood and into adulthood, the two of us have never forgotten that story. It's my one ace in the hole against my dad. Whenever I want to make him feel bad, in a joking, loving, spiteful sort of way, all I have to do is bring up the special child story and voila! Vindication.

And in that story about Abraham, or Moses, or whoever that guy was who freed slaves, I also learned about pride. I was so very sure of myself when I announced to my family that I knew who Abraham Lincoln was. I was wrong. With my family's laughter, and my tender age, I didn't really have to swallow that pride, but I did have to sip it down in little gulps.

Today, my father knows that he taught me a lesson in humility because he truly was able to come to his six-year-old daughter to apologize to her for something he admitted doing wrong; what he doesn't know is that this was only one lesson on one topic and that both he and my mom would spend a lifetime teaching me more. But whatever you do, please, please don't tell my dad how well I learned the lesson about humility because now that he's eighty-five, the guilt card is the only good one I have to play when he beats the pants off of me at gin rummy.

Two Hairs Passed a Freckle

When I was a little girl, and I'd asked my dad what time it was, he'd respond by telling me that it was two hairs passed a freckle. He'd smile with that certain endearing smile. It's the one that exuded love and a sense of humor at the same time, and it was always accompanied by the slant of his eyes, one always had an extra twinkle as if to say this light's for you. Enjoy it while you can.

The passage of time marched on whether I wanted it to or not. I grew up. I found myself in a grown up life with grown up responsibilities. In the morning, I checked the oven clock to make sure we left in time to catch the train. At work, I checked the computer to make sure I didn't miss the meeting. In the car, I checked the dashboard to see how long I was stuck in traffic, and on the fly, I checked my phone to see if I was on schedule. But none of them had a face with the sides of a mouth that curved upward when I asked them the time. None of them responded with love and humor at the same time, and none of them had eyes that twinkled at me full of wisdom as the minutes passed telling me that there was a light there, just for me.

When I raised my own children, we had our cherished moments. We had our traditions. I taught them how to tie their shoes. I taught them how to read. I answered their questions when they asked me if we were there yet or if they could stay out passed curfew. When they asked me where they came from, I tried to tell them. When they asked what compassion was, I tried to show them. But dad, I forgot how to answer them properly when they asked me what time it was. I forgot to stop and show them the importance of a little sense of humor. I forgot to look at them with love and humor at the same time. I forgot to put that extra twinkle in my eye just for them. I forgot what time it was.

So Dad, please do me a favor since I forgot. Would you please call my kids and tell them to ask me what time it is? There's still time. I know there is - because it's still two hairs passed a freckle, Dad - it's still two hairs.

Dog Lovers of America Unite

Remember the old game show Password? The TV viewer was the audience who heard the emcee whisper out the answer to the current clue being given. The players each had partners to whom they would have to give a clue in an attempt to get them to give them the winning answer.

Let's say the answer is "lamp." A typical game went something like this:

Player 1A giving a clue to his partner Player 1B:

"Light."

Player 1B giving an answer to Player 1A:

"Bulb."

Now it's the other team's turn.

Player 2A giving a clue to his partner Player 2B:

"Shade."

Now Player 2B gives the winning answer to Player 2A:

"Lamp."

The "B" team wins the round.

And so goes the game of Password. There was a home version. It was a board game without the board. The game came in a box with cards that had answers on them. The players would team up and give clues to their partners in order to get them to give the correct answer.

We tried playing this game in my house when my kids were growing up, but it never worked out. I blame the dogs. We've always had two dogs (although now we have three). If you were to call us dog lovers, it would be a gross understatement. We're the crazy people who stop you on the street when you're trying to give your dog a quick walk before work. We have to stop you. We can't help ourselves. We have to bend down and look your pup in the face and talk baby talk to him. We have to pet him, and kiss him on his mouth, and tell him how cute he is. Sometimes, we might even look at you and thank you for taking care of such a precious being.

So perhaps now you'll understand why we can no longer play password in my family. Here's what happened.

My husband and one of my girls made up one team. My other daughter and I made up the other team. My team took the first turn. It was I who was giving the first clue to my daughter. The super-secret answer was "trousers." So if you're following me, you will understand that I'm trying to give my daughter clues to get her to say the word "trousers."

I calmly clear my throat. I look her straight in the eye, and I give her the following, very reasonable clue:

"Pants."

She was so excited when she gave me her immediate response. She was sure she got the answer on the first try. Her response:

"Dog."

We've never tried playing Password since.

Chapter Two: Marriage and The Baby Carriage

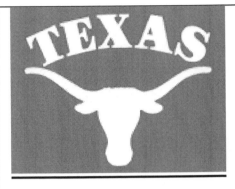

From Cornell to The University of Texas

To me, your twenties and thirties should be some of your best years. Mine were no exception. I was off to college. I went to the University of Texas to study Journalism/Public Relations. But I had continued to work in hotels and by the time my sophomore year rolled around, I thought that perhaps, I should be majoring in hotel management. Cornell was a top notch school for such a program. So I went to see the school for a weekend of touring and interviewing. As it happened, I was the little sister for a fraternity at UT, so I had our president call the president of the their chapter at Cornell to see if he knew of a place that I could stay while on campus for the weekend. The fraternity was small, and for extra income, they rented out a few floors as female residences. In no time, I was flying to Cornell, getting a tour, participating in an interview, and meeting a lovely gal who took the time to show me the ropes. By Saturday afternoon of that weekend, Charlotte, my new girlfriend, took me down to the rec room to meet two of her friends. I met a guy whose name I cannot remember. The other guy's name was Martin. So the four of us sat down to converse and play a game of cards together. Several hours later, and after numerous games, neither I, nor Martin, could take our eyes off of one another. If it hadn't happened to me, I wouldn't have believed it, but it was absolutely, positively, love at first sight.

We spent that evening going to a hockey game. Martin said he'd catch the puck for me. He did. The next day, he called his mom and told her he met the girl he was going to marry. He put me on a plane to fly back home to Texas. The man sitting next to me on the plane told me I looked like I'd just left the love of my life. I looked that man straight in the eyes and told him I had.

Three and a half years later, Marty and I (I renamed him because I thought Martin was a geeky name, and my guy was anything but geeky) were married and shortly after that, we had two beautiful baby girls. So now, I shared my life with this wonderful new man and his family, my two girls, my brother, my parents, and of course, we got a dog.

Fairies

Did you know that married men are followed by fairies everywhere they go? Take the car, for instance. When it breaks down, the first thing my husband does is get out of the vehicle and look under the hood. I can tell you as a matter of the utmost fact that he hasn't got the first clue as to what he's looking at but, nonetheless, he has to pop that hood and take a look inside. For the longest time I couldn't understand it. I knew that he had no knowledge whatsoever about cars except where to put the gas, and even then, I had to remind him which side of the pump to pull up to. But now, I have finally figured it out. Popping the hood is the official male sign language for "please pull over and help before my wife finds out I'm clueless." This male-only language works like a charm. Sure enough, within minutes, a strange single man will pull over, school my husband on the problem, and drive off into the sunset. My husband will then close the hood, get back in the car, and call AAA. When I dare to ask what the problem is, he responds by telling me that it, of course, is the gasket and that the car will have to be towed. "Well what did that guy say that stopped?" I ask. " Oh he just told me I was right." So where's the fairy you ask? Well she's sitting in the passenger seat pretending she believes in his extensive car knowledge.

But that's just the car fairy. Married men have other fairies too. There's the toilet paper fairy, the one who always makes sure there's a roll available when needed. There's the cream fairy, who always makes sure there is enough cream in the fridge for coffee. My favorite is the tool fairy. My sweet spouse has never been very handy around the house. We recently bought a new home and he's been trying to be the fixit man all by himself. I must give him credit; he's actually fixed a few things. It took him thirty-four years and three drills, however. You see, each time he would go to use the drill over the years, we didn't yet have a tool fairy. So, inevitably, he could never find the drill, its charger, or the bits that went with it. Thus the next time he needed a drill, he would go out and buy a new one. Well once I discovered drill #3 in the house, I found the tool fairy. She makes sure that the drill gets to go back in the little case where it lives after a fair day's work. She's actually one of my best finds ever. Now when my husband decides to get handy and asks me where his drill is, I can tell him with confidence that it's in its case where it lives. Go tool fairy!

As for me, I appreciate the fairies in the house. They're so efficient, reliable, and cost- effective. But somehow, they make me very tired. The more fairies my husband gets, the more tired I become. Perhaps this is why the tooth fairy hasn't been around for a while. She was busy when our kids were little, but now that they're all grown up, she's taking a break. Thank goodness my husband doesn't need her, at least not as long as his appointment fairy keeps making him dentist appointments.

You know, the tooth fairy is the only fairy who gets paid? I've gotta find out where she got her fairy degree because with mine, I have yet to get a pay check.

The Eyes of a Child

I am not a pervert. No really. I swear. I just want to look into the eyes of your child. I want to see into his beautiful soul. I want to inhale his youth and innocence. I want to protect his well-being.

I never knew how much I adored children until I had two of my own. Like any mother, I doted over them, overprotected them, cherished them, and thought that unlike your children, mine could walk on water.

But soon, I found myself surrounded by my friends' children. After that, I found myself surrounded by my children's friends. That's when I made my discovery: I adored children. I wanted to adopt them all. I didn't care how old they were. I didn't care what they looked like. I just wanted to soak in their goodness and make sure that it was protected. I would eye their caregivers until I felt comfortable that the children were safe in their hands. These children, to me, were the most sacred thing on Earth and were to be protected, loved, and cherished at any expense.

Of course I favored my own children over all others. I am a mother after all. But once my own children were born, something sparked within my very being that made me want to take on the role of mother of all children. I wanted to look into their eyes and see into their futures. Were their caregivers loving enough? Did they have proper nutrition and shelter? Were they getting a good education? Were they getting just the right amount of discipline...not too strict, but with enough boundaries and structure?

I felt it was my personal business to cherish every child I saw. I wanted to walk up to every single child I saw and give them a big squeeze and tell them that I loved them. I wanted to give them my phone number and tell them that if they were ever in trouble to call me, and I would come and help them.

For a long time, I thought I should have gone back to school to become a teacher. As much as I adored the children that came across my path, I had to force myself to come to the realization that if I acted upon all those instincts, people would think I was a pedophile. At the very least, they would think I was some kind of pervert. I have to admit that if someone tried to approach one of my children the way I felt like approaching others', we'd have a serious and immediate issue on our hands with the local police, the state police, and the FBI.

So I tamed my passion on my own children forcing myself not to be a helicopter mom. I forced myself to let go of them a little at a time, and allow them to rise, and fall, and get back up again. I used my powers of inner strength to admire others' children at a distance so as not to scare either the child or his guardian. I stopped myself from going back to school to study education because I knew that the love I would pour over my students would be misconstrued as something less innocent than it was.

But to this day, when I see a child, any child, anywhere, I admire them. I cherish them. I wish for them to keep their pure souls into adulthood and to spread them to their children. Because there is nothing, nothing in this world, more precious than a child.

A Squeeze in the Middle

I'm a squeezer. I squeeze in the middle. Give me a brand new tube of toothpaste, and the first thing I do is squeeze it right in the middle. What comes out, is the perfect portion, the perfect squeeze. It fits just right on my toothbrush as it enters my mouth cleaning my teeth with the perfect balance of exfoliating minty goodness. It's restorative. It is refreshing.

When my daughter was two, I would scoop her up in my arms placing them just so under her butt so that I created the perfect seat for her. She would comfortably put her left arm around my neck and her right on the back of my shoulder. She had the habit of taking that right hand and assuredly patting me on my shoulder: pat, pat, pat, before it rested there. Then her little index finger would crook in the middle and be implanted in her mouth self-pacifying her with the sucking of her not yet outgrown infancy. This, after she'd already comforted me with the pat, pat, pat of her little two-year-old hand on my shoulder.

I'd give her a squeeze to comfort her right back. She would turn her plump precious lips to my cheek and kiss it with a "mwah" sound emanating from her very being followed by a hug back that included an "ouh" sound, her way of offering up a physical and verbal kiss and a hug. It was the squeeze and the "mwah ouh" that really mattered. When we squeezed each other, it was in the middle, like the toothpaste: all the best parts would come out before we moved on to the rest of our daily routine.

When she got a little older, and I could no longer make my arms into a seat for her, I would bend down to her. She could still wrap her left arm around my neck and her right around my shoulder. Gone was the pat, pat, pat to reassure me. Gone was the crooked index finger inserted in her mouth to pacify her. It was replaced by my arms wrapped back around her middle with a squeeze and a "mwah ouh" from each of us. It was her way of reminding me that I could rest assured she still loved me, and it was my way of reassuring her that I'd be there when she got home, and that school, and play dates, and big girl things were good things to do without me there.

By the time she was old enough to go off to sleep away camp, I no longer had to bend down to meet her, but the arms were there: we were entwined, wrapped around each other, always with a squeeze in the middle to get at the best part and always accompanied by "mwah ouh" before we parted for the summer weeks ahead.

College came and went. The years flashed by. I can remember visualizing the camera bulbs of my generation in the snap shots and snippets I saw of her college days. There were flashes of light, followed by momentary darkness. The darkness blinded my eyes from the bright light that shadowed the moments I missed sharing with her as I forced myself to let her grow up. Then the bulbs were burned and ejected from the camera, but the memories were still emblazoned in the photos of the days gone by. But always, always, before we parted, there was the squeeze in the middle and the "mwah ouh."

Some days, I go to the grocery, and I see other mothers with their children. The mothers are hurried with life and its challenges. The children sit in their plastic and metal shopping carts with no arms to make them a seat. Their tiny little hands wrap around a teddy bear or a favorite blanket. I see a finger on one hand in their mouth and the other hand holding onto their " lovey" with a pat, pat, pat. I too, suffered those harried days of errands, and work, and the stresses of life. I am so very grateful that I was able to take time out to receive the assurance of the pat, pat, pat from the wisdom of my two-year-old. I am so grateful that I was able to return it with a squeeze: the squeeze that pushed out all the good stuff.

Today, we never see each other enough, but not a phone call gets made, not an e-mail gets sent, not a text goes out, without our saying to each other "mwah ouh" before we sign off. I can't always feel the squeeze in person now, but it's there. It's there with the perfect balance of a hug and a kiss, and when it oozes out of the tube, it's restorative and refreshing.

Their Eyes, They are a Rollin'

They're rolling their eyes at me again. They just don't understand. I've been making a very strong effort over the past year to be better. I have been better. But they don't see my improvement. They still roll their eyes way into the backs of their heads. They roll them the way I told them not to when they were growing up. I told them to stop doing it because they would get stuck that way and they would never again be able to see out of the front of their faces. But they didn't listen then, and they don't listen now.

The rolling is due to the fact that I have once again made some comment, about saving some item, for some day, for some child, that I may at some time call my grandchild.

Ok, they're still young. Of course I want them to enjoy their careers and their youth. Of course I want them to get married first. Of course I want them to be financially able. But honestly, is it such a crime for a Jewish mother who's been an empty nester for several years now, to want the joy of grandmotherhood?

When my kids were little, I used to always say that there were three things a mom had to do to prove to me that she was a good mom. She had to:

1) be ready and willing to spit on anything-spit on your thumb to wipe the chocolate off her kids' face, spit on their swim goggles so they wouldn't fog up, or spit on the pull string of their coat so she could thread the end that's lost its cover back through the eyelet.

2) go to the bathroom in a public stall with the stall door open. (Well you don't expect her to leave the kid alone in the stroller on the other side of the door now do you?)

and

3) fish at least one item per child out of a toilet bowl.

Gone are the days of my trying to prove I was a good mom. Gone are my mornings waking up to a warm little body crawling up under the covers with me on a cold winter day. Gone are my peaceful nights reading their favorite bedtime story to them for the second time. Gone are the squeezes

I got around my neck on a daily basis, and gone are the scraps of paper covering my fridge with artwork finer than any you can see at the MOMA.

Yes, of course, gone too are the days of worrying, screaming, cajoling, and counseling. But I just don't remember those days very much.

So please forgive me my rolley-eyed children while I anxiously await the day I can call myself a grandma because that will be the beginning of not only the days I wish for myself, but the days I wish for you!

True Tales/Tails of Our Silly Family

You've read about my family's games of Oh Rats and Password. Now come along and play one with me. Come on. Be a sport. It'll put a smile on your face, so why not? Maybe you'll even be able to say you won.

This is a story about my adventures as a writer with homophones, not to be confused with homophobes, which is a whole other walk down the aisle. So I'll tell you a little about what I mean when I talk about my adventures with homophones.

Homophones are two or more words which sound identical but are spelled differently and have different meanings. An example is the following: "oar," "or," and "ore." How many can you identify as you learn about my adventures with them?

My exploits began with the old story we used to tell in my family, about a poor family that immigrated to the United States from a little isle in the sea off the coast of Greece. They had to flee the country in a hurry to take advantage of a job offer in America. Once they settled and started to become financially able, they sent care packages home to their loved ones in Europe. Their European family members could not always understand the labels on the tins sent from America, but they were always grateful for the supplies. They would brush off an occasional flea and sometimes an ant crawling on top of the box and happily open the gifts inside. (Are you still with me and counting the homophones?)

On one such occasion, a package arrived for the family in Europe with a letter to follow a day or two later. The family eagerly opened the package and began consuming the treats inside. One unmarked tin was a complete mystery. When the family opened the tin, they found it to contain a light colored powder, and promptly added water and boiled up a tasty pot of soup with a little bacon grease for added flavor. It was delicious. The letter came four days later. It stated the American family's sorrow over the loss of Aunt Mary and explained that her ashes were enclosed in the tin in the care package. When Mary's niece read the letter, the poor thing went insane and ran screaming through the neighborhood "I ate my Aunt! I ate my Aunt"! It was horrible. It was funny. It was horrible.

The family eventually got over the incident and went to bury Aunt Mary's ashes. Other packages continued to arrive from America, the weight of one always heavier than the last, full of jams, canned meat, and sometimes a different kind of berry or two. One package came with eight different types of cheese. But after the incident with the ashes, they would always wait to meet the mailman looking for any follow up letters before they ate any of the goodies inside.

I'm full of many other stories that my family used to tell. When my kids were little and we would take long drives down the dusty roads of Texas, we often saw cows and a bale or two of hay on the side of the road. From the silent car, one of us would always yell out "hey" to get a reaction. We'd always wait to see who would say "what?" and fall for the joke. It was always funny. Had you really seen hay or did you just shout out "hey" to get the desired response? Invariably, one of us always fell for the joke.

One of my fondest memories of my grandfather was the time he came home exasperated telling us that the weather was too bad and too icy for the toll taker to be trying to have a conversation with the drivers that went through her booth that day. When we looked him in the eye and asked him what on earth he was talking about, he told us that he threw his money in the toll basket, then the toll taker said "I see spots." Grandpa said it was just ridiculous. He told her that if she was seeing spots, that she should go see her doctor. He turned beet red when we told him that the toll taker was just trying to be nice when she gave out the warning that there were "icy spots" on the road.

I must tell you something about all these stories. They're all completely true. In full disclosure, I don't know if the story about the family in Europe is true, but the fact that we used to tell it when I was growing up, is completely true – so, too, is the story about hay and my Grandpa's "icy spots." I will now leave you in peace about this piece on homophones so that no one arrests me and I have to have my husband come bail me out.

The following homophones were used in this essay: (Did you find them all, or did you get tied up in a knot?)

tale/tail

not/knot

won/one

Greece/grease

eight/ate

bury/berry

meat/meet

hay/hey

peace/piece

through/threw

aisle/isle/I'll

too/two/to

oar/or/ore

sea/see

flee/flea

their/they're/there

ant/aunt

bale/bail

read/red

weight/wait

for/four

…and I'm counting "icy" and "I see" because I can.

Chapter Three: My Glass Gets Empty, but I Refill It

Surviving Disasters

I was a late bloomer boomer. In other words, I almost can't identify with boomers born in the late forties and fifties. By the time I got to college, most women who had the means, went to college and planned careers. I never really quite fit in. Although I was pursuing a degree in journalism and public relations, and though I was working in hotels all through college and after graduation, I desperately wanted a family of my own. When we were finally ready to have children, I felt that age old pull that all women have: the one in which we have to decide on the right balance of career and family. My pull was totally toward family. I wanted to be a stay-at-home mom. I wanted the nice house, the nice cars, the nice vacations, and I wanted my husband home by six o'clock every night. This was the mid-eighties and that just wasn't realistic. So I began to be an on and off working mom. When the girls were babies, I was fortunate enough to have Marty as the most supportive husband a woman could ever have. He was willing to work with me on being able to stay home with them, and he even put up with my demands for him to get home from work at a decent hour and then change a diaper or two to boot. If I did nothing else right in my life, I'd be ok with that because I am one of the few women in this world that can actually say that walking down the aisle to marry my guy of choice was the best thing I have ever done.

You'll be able to see this for yourself when I painfully divulge to you in the next few essays how shameful I felt when I wasn't as supportive to him, as he has always been to me. We've survived job loss and financial strain together. We've survived Marty stepping out of the World Trade Center in New York City on the morning of September 11, 2001. We've survived cancer together. We've survived it over, and over, and over.

My glass, admittedly, has been empty. It's been bone dry. But then, as you will read, I witness a stranger who doesn't even have a glass. Then, I am grateful, and my glass fills right back up again.

Tears

There was screaming. Doors were slamming shut. Tears were coming down. But these weren't just any tears. They looked different. When you laugh, you get the kind that puddle up in the corners of your eyes and you wipe them away with the palm of your hand and a chuckle in your belly. When you're sad, you get the kind that roll down your cheek flowing freely. They drip down your collar and snot up your nose. No. These were different. These were tears of shame and embarrassment. These were tears that didn't want to puddle or roll. These were tears that didn't want to come out at all but couldn't help themselves as they reluctantly dripped sideways into the hairline instead of following gravity down the face. These were my tears.

When Marty and I first met, sparks flew, physical attraction bloomed, and we couldn't get enough of one another. I can clearly remember the amazing feeling I had when all we did was look at each other and quiver with delight. Fresh in my mind are the days when just the scent of him was enough to send my mind into outer space. We had an abundance of passion for one another. For me, this passion was something I had never experienced before. I wanted to cherish it. It was something I shared with Marty and no one else. I don't want to ever share it with anyone else. It's ours and ours alone: his and mine. It's near and dear and always there.

Ok, you may say, but that was thirty-four years ago, hasn't that passion faded over time? Don't you feel the desire for that passion again? My answer to both questions is yes, yes, of course. But I found something even better. I found in Marty a never ending well of love, trust, and support. I have the most implicit trust in my husband. He could tell me he's spending the weekend with a female friend from high school and I would tell him to have a great time. Without asking, I know he would react the same way with me.

Even after three plus decades of marriage, we do still have a physical attraction to one another, even though we are two not such good looking people, we're still in love. Have you ever stopped to wonder why two not such good looking people can get together? Have you ever had that momentary nauseating thought of the two of your parents in bed together? YUK! Marty and I don't have perfect bodies. We're not young, we don't have hard core abs and rock hard biceps. I've had two babies for god sakes that left me with a flabby mess of loose skin around my middle.

Years ago, after the birth of both our girls, Marty and I were in bed together. He went to put his arm around my waist. I flinched. He was taken aback. Why would I flinch at his touch? As I explained it to him, I had never had this unpleasant loose skin around my middle before. I was very self-conscious about it. I didn't want him to feel it. He turned to me and looked me straight in the eye and told me that he liked it. He liked it? He said it just reminded him of our two beautiful girls that we made together. My flab was a part of him as much as it was a part of me. I melted.

We were young then. Life happened. I got really sick. We both got really sad. We cried. We shed the sad tears, the one's that flow freely down your cheek and make your nose all snotty.

It was one more thing we shared together. We supported each other in sickness and in health. Until one of us didn't.

More life happened, and one day, we both found ourselves out of work. Marty told me that he had always had a desire to become a trader on the stock exchange. I listened to him pour his heart out to me about how he felt he had a passion for it and wanted to give it a try. He explained to me that from everything he had learned about it, no one really made money doing it during their first year in business. "What do you mean you won't be making any money," I said? I was anything but supportive. His mind was made up. He was going to give this a try. This is when the screaming started. I was doing the screaming. This is when the doors started slamming shut. I did the slamming. I was angry. I was unsupportive. I had lost my way.

More life happened. This time it was 9/11. Yep, he was right in the thick of it that day- right there at Ground Zero. He managed to get a call through to me to tell me to turn on the TV and to tell me he was ok. Then we got disconnected as the first tower fell. It had been a beautiful day-warm and clear, but I began to sweat. I felt like the glue stick someone had just shot out of a heated glue gun. This putrid oozing feeling leaked out of my pores. Where was my husband? Was he ok?

At three o'clock that afternoon, he came walking into the house. He was covered with white sooty debris, but he was walking. He was alive! I cried. But this time they were the tears of shame and embarrassment. They were the tears that didn't want to puddle or roll. These were the tears that didn't want to come out at all but couldn't help themselves as they reluctantly dripped sideways into the hairline instead of following gravity down the face. How could I have been so unsupportive of this man who had spent his life supporting me in every way imaginable? This time, we didn't share the tears. This time, they were mine.

Years later, there was Super Storm Sandy. We had all lost power for several days. My ninety-year-old mother-in-law included. We were the first in the family to get power back. I made a beeline for North Jersey to pick up my mother-in-law and her aide and get them out of their 35°F apartment and into my warm home. Understand that both my mother-in-law and her aide were about the least two demanding people I knew. Nonetheless, we were all there in our tiny little rental house with one bathroom. Mom's wheelchair didn't fit in the bathroom so we spent a few days with the bathroom door removed so we could get her in and out as necessary. No matter how easy they both were to get along with, it was still a stressful time. The wheelchair alone took up half my living room. There was nowhere to turn around. When we heard that power had been restored to their apartment, we were all happy to get back to our normal living arrangements. It was noon before I could load them up in the car and get them back to their home. After dropping them off, I had to meet with a realtor. We were in the midst of losing our house as a result of the mortgage crisis and had a window of opportunity to try to sell it first. It was election day and I was anxious to get home to vote before the polls closed. When I finally finished my business with the realtor, it was after 5pm. It normally took me about an hour and a half to drive home without traffic, and I was sure the polls closed at 7. I was a wreck. We'd had several stressful days with the living arrangement, it was stressful to have to put the house on the market because we could no longer afford it, and I had never missed voting in a presidential election in my life. The traffic was relentless. I was going nuts. All my stress came out in anger. I don't know who I was angry at. I was just angry. I wanted to bite someone's head off. I'd never make it home before the polls closed. Marty was waiting in the driveway for me when I pulled up to our rental. He told me not to panic. The polling place was less than a mile away and they were open until 8. I was relieved but I was still angry. I was angry at the day, angry at the stress. And then Marty said just two words to me, just two. "Thank you". He thanked me. He was thanking me for helping with his mom whom I had always loved anyway, and he was thanking me for taking care of the business with the realtor. With those two words, the stress and the anger in my body came to an abrupt halt like a thunderstorm when the rain suddenly stops and the sun comes out. I was washed clean and able to shine again.

Marty does this to me. He's not romantic. He never was. He doesn't get me gifts for my birthday. He never did. (He and I still need to talk about this issue). But he's my rock. He's my lover and my confidant. I don't know how I could ever live without him.

No, it's been many years since we've had that passion of whirlwind attraction that we had when we first met. We have moments. Sometimes the moments are every day for several in a row. Sometimes the moments are months apart. But they're moments that I share with him and only him. I wouldn't want it any other way.

We are, neither of us perfect. He procrastinates until I can't stand it anymore and do whatever it is myself. I clean up neurotically needing everything to be at just the right angle and in just the right place. But we match somehow.

Marty doesn't believe in PDA's, public displays of affection. Me, I could care less. Let the whole world be jealous that I'm loving my husband in front of them, at least to a point. But we hold hands frequently. I adore his hands. They wrap around mine just so. They fit. Sometimes, I'll grab his hand and he doesn't seem to even respond. But sometimes I'll grab it and he gives it a little squeeze. I know he's there for me. I cherish the squeeze.

We share boring days and happy days, and we still shed tears - we shed them together. But nowadays they're the kind that puddle up in the corners of your eyes, and you wipe them away with the palm of your hand and a chuckle in your belly.

Perfection

They say that nothing is perfect. They are wrong.

Perfection exists. I have found it. It's brief, and it's fleeting, but it exists. It exists in the dark of the night. I have found it lying next to the warm musk of the man I love in that darkness. I can't see him in the stillness of the night and the barrier of the pillows, but I can feel him, and I can hear him. I feel the rough hairs on his chest that were non-existent when we met. I hear the soft tenor of his voice that has a slight gravel from age. We talk through the stillness sharing the history of our lives. Only those with decades of history have this shared commonality. We talk of the past. We talk of the present. We talk of the future...our future. Some of the best parts are the parts left unsaid, the mute moments when we are both thinking the same thoughts and we know it. Then it comes from nowhere...the comment that makes me laugh. It's the one only the two of us will understand. Only we share that laughter, privately, in the darkness, the laughter shaking the bed uncontrollably. Then the laughter actually escalates when he knows my bladder will not comply with my will to keep it in check...the bladder that has weakened from birthing babies and aging.

I don't believe in God, but if I did, this laughter would be the closest thing one must be able to get to Him. It's not the laughter of the mocking of another nor the one giggle from a cute Facebook post. It's the laughter of decades of understanding and history shared with one another. It may launch love making, exhaustion, and sleep, but before it does, it defines perfection...a fleeting moment in the dark and the warmth of his familiar scent, we share the laughter.

The sunlight of the morning comes. The routine of life resumes. Those fleeting moments end, but in them, I found perfection. Perfection exists. I know. I've felt it wrapped in years of love, respect, and laughter...most of all, laughter.

Again

My dad pulled in to the drug store parking lot, and I waited uncomfortably in the car while he went in to fill the prescription. In an attempt to get comfortable, I put my feet up on the dash — a terrible habit I've had since childhood. The numbness was wearing off, and the throbbing was starting. It was bad this time.

I'd had numerous biopsies. Fortunately, they all came back benign. But this one, for some reason, was particularly bad. Perhaps I was just raw from all the previous unhealed spots.

I wriggled in my seat, half-choking myself as the seat belt cut across my throat. I sunk way down, twisting and searching for a comfortable way to plant myself deep into the roots of the car.

A surge of pain came, as fast as the cars whizzing by on the main road behind the parking lot. Another came right behind, tailgating much too closely. Then it slammed into me. I kicked the windshield of my dad's Mercedes, and it cracked with a loud "BOOM!" followed by the slow spread of pain snaking through my whole body.

Dad made it back to the car, prescription in hand, shocked to find both me and his car is such poor condition. We drove home. I took the pain killers. They didn't kill the pain.

A few days later, we got the good news: The biopsy had come back benign again.

That had been the worst biopsy so far. I went through several years of more benign results. And then the phone call finally came — it was malignant. I officially had tongue cancer. It's common in smokers, older men, and heavy drinkers. I was none of these.

We went to Memorial Sloan-Kettering Hospital to sign a bunch of papers. They patiently placed one after another in front of me to sign. I remember thinking that I should read what I was signing but that it didn't really matter. I needed the surgery. I had to sign them anyway.

I was worried. I'd already been dealing with this for five or six years. I was always in so much pain from the biopsies. This time it was really cancer. How was I going to manage so much pain?

After the surgery, they sent me to a pain-management specialist, who gave me lots of drugs. They never really killed the pain, but they did take the edge off. After that first surgery in 1998, it all became a blurred, continuous loop of biopsies, malignancies and surgeries for another 10 years. So many, I've lost count.

I went for check-ups every 90 days. I hated even the good check-ups, because each one meant a two-hour commute back to the hospital's head and neck department. I'd often wait for an hour in the office, trying hard to think about how lucky I was as I stared at people with half a face and listened to the amplifiers of people who no longer had vocal chords. Then I'd get 15 minutes of poking and prodding into my most sensitive physical and emotional place, followed by a two-hour train ride back home filled with throbbing pain, every dent in the track a jolt of lightning to my mouth.

Then came another bad check-up — the usual word "malignant," but this time accompanied by the words "aggressive type." The doctors explained that this time I would have more than emotional scars. They would have to take more of the tongue, part of the jaw, some teeth, and they would have to do a neck dissection — a scar from the middle of my throat to the back of my ear.

In 2010, I experienced a series of bouts that never gave me more than six months of reprieve between malignancies. That's when I built up a tolerance for the narcotics and needed more and more to take that edge off.

One day, I told the pain-management doc that I was in a lot less pain and wanted to get off all of the drugs. It was like poking my head out of a drug-induced cloud to see a little bit of blue sky. To my amazement, she congratulated me and sent me on my way, nary a prescription in hand. A few days later, I was out of drugs completely, and less than 24 hours later, withdrawal ensued.

I called the doctor to explain what was happening and to ask for more medication so that I could wean myself more gradually, but they told me that they could no longer prescribe medication because I had told them I was not in as much pain.

Severe psychological agitation transitioned quickly to severe physical agitation. I had the chills and the sweats at the same time. The same foot that went through my dad's windshield a few years earlier was now kicking off covers, blankets, and pillows. I wanted everything off. I wanted the noise in my head to turn off. I pulled and twisted my face like the figure in the Edvard Munch's "The Scream."

With time and my husband's nurturing, it eventually faded away. I emerged from the fog whole. The physical pain never completely left, and the emotional pain was stored forever in my memory. But at least I could think clearly again.

Within six months, the cancer was back. I had lost count — was this surgery number nine or number ten? I couldn't survive it without pain meds. I forced myself to go back to the pain doctor. This time the cocktail was a mix of Morphine and Fentanyl.

The cancer returned again, and again, until finally there was a break. I was nine months cancer free, and although I was never free from pain, I wanted to be free from that fog.

I was a bit older and a lot wiser. I knew that if I could kick pain killers once, I could kick them again. With my patient husband by my side, I weaned myself off of everything for the second time in my life. This time it was much easier. This time I did it my way. I cancelled my pain doctor appointments, and I haven't been back since.

I've now had the fortune of being free of cancer for three years — the longest break of my 20-year saga. At a check-up nine months ago, the doc actually said for the first time that "It might not come back!" Instead of giving me an appointment to come back in 90 days, he told me not to come back for six months.

I told my folks the good news. When I repeated what the doctor told me, I said "might," but they, ever hopeful, heard "won't."

When I went for that follow-up visit, there was a new pre-cancerous spot brewing. I knew it was there. It had been hurting me. I was back to my regular check-up routine. The last time I saw my doc, we both knew it was bigger.

It's coming back, but slowly. Next time I'll be ready for it, because next time I'll know a few things. I'll know I might get three years before I have to go through it again. I'll know I can kick the drugs when I want my life back, and I'll know car windshields can be mended, and so can damaged tongues.

A Quart of Milk

I went to the Wawa with my husband to pick up a quart of milk. As we parked the car, we noticed a young man passed out and lying in front of the store.

"That guy's not doing too well," my husband said.

I agreed and we went about our business, not at all compelled to do or say anything further.

Leaving with the milk, I again noticed the man in front of the store. This time, there was a police SUV pulled up at an angle, lights flashing in the parking lot. And this time, I really saw the man. He was in such an awkward position. It looked as if his upper body wouldn't hold him up anymore, and it just fell over at a ninety-degree angle, leaving his lower body just where he had left it. A police officer was rummaging in the guy's pockets. I assumed he was looking for drugs, an ID, or both.

When the cop pulled him somewhat into a sitting position, I saw that the young man was alive and awake. I noticed his eyes for the first time. They were beautiful, soft, like there was a kind soul behind them. But they scared me. They were looking out at nothing. He was so out of it, he wasn't responding at all.

Buckling up in the car, I could see his eyes better. I could see right through them, but they couldn't see me. A shiver went down my spine.

The man was filthy, like he hadn't had a bath in a month. His hair was greasy. His face was so dirty I almost couldn't tell the color of his skin. His jeans looked like he'd worn them for a year and never once washed them. They fit him well. At some point long ago, he must have tried them on, looked in a mirror, and decided they looked good on him. Maybe he bought them nearby.

Beyond the filth, and beyond the eyes, he looked like a very nice-looking young man in his early twenties. When we pulled up, we hadn't really noticed him. Just a bum passed out. But now, I saw almost a boy.

As we pulled away from the parking lot, I wondered out loud where the cop would take him. I figured he was taking him to jail. We left with the mutual understanding that it was none of our business.

The next night, I couldn't stop thinking about that guy - his beautiful eyes and his good looks. It made me sad to think of him in jail. Of course, he was probably on something illegal, but he wasn't hurting anyone but himself. What good would jail do him? How was he the next morning? Did they let him go? Where? Why was he on the sidewalk in front of the Wawa, right there and right then for me to cross his path? And why didn't I care when I first saw him? For all we knew, he could have been dead.

In my youth, he would have disgusted me. I would have called him a low-life and been appalled at the waste. But now, in my older years, I've seen more, experienced more. I know what things can happen to people. I have more compassion.

I know I can't go out there and save the world, that there are people without homes, with mental illness and addiction, all over the country. But who was this guy? Whose best buddy was he in high school? Whose son is he? Is he a brother, a father, a boyfriend? Does anyone know where he is or why he didn't call? Does anyone care?

So I decided I'd march myself down to the police station in the morning. I couldn't tell my husband. He'd think I was crazy and tell me not to get involved. I actually didn't want to get involved. I had no tools to help this man. I didn't even know if the police would share any information with me whatsoever. I only wanted to know where they took him, what may have happened to him, and if there was any chance he could have received any help.

Because, now, he'd crossed my path. Now, I needed to know.

The next morning, I visited the station. I explained why I was there and what I wanted. I felt like an idiot. Who was I to ask? What right did I have to any information? The clerk was very polite. I'm sure she thought it odd that I would stop in to inquire.

She really couldn't give me any specific information. There are privacy laws. She did tell me, to my relief, that it was unlikely that he was taken to jail, that more likely the officer took him to the hospital. Once treated, she said, he would have been released and left on his own.

She said there is help available for people like him, but he has to ask for it. I hope he asks. I went to the police station looking for comfort. I found none. Perhaps he will find some.

So now I know-at least as much as I'm entitled to know, which is basically nothing. In this free country we live in, America, our nation, I find myself grateful - grateful that I am free from a dictator and grateful that I am free from addiction. I hope that man finds his way. I hope that one day he, too, will go for a quart of milk. I hope that when he does, I'll know that he has once again crossed my path, only this time, he'll be free, and I will want to know.

A Thank You Note

You. Yes, you. You and every human being you know need to send my husband a personal thank you note. It should be hand written, double spaced, and addressed to "the amazing spouse of Leslie Handler." Why you ask? Why should you owe him a thank you note? Well here's the reason.

For thirty-four years we've lived together. And for thirty-four years my dear husband has accepted the fate of being the husband of a Jewish wife. Now if you know nothing else about Jewish wives, you must know this. They are experts in two things: guilt and suffering. Now don't go thinking that I'm generalizing here because I'm not. I freely admit that there are Jewish women who are amazing professionals, homemakers, intellectuals, and philanthropists. There are Jewish women who are doctors, lawyers, chefs, and accountants. None of us can do it all. But all of us do guilt and suffering.

Some of us can even do them at the very same time. There is evidence of this in a classic Jewish joke.

Question: How many Jewish women does it take to change a light bulb?

Answer: It's alright, I'll sit in the dark.

You see? Guilt and suffering at the same time.

So what does this have to do with my husband and the thank you note you need to write to him? In order to answer, you need to know about my personal suffering. I've suffered the little things, and I've suffered some of the big ones. I've suffered rejection from the college of my choice, not being a member of the "in" crowd, car accidents, job losses, skipping a meal (but only one, I had the flu and it was Yom Kippur), losing my wallet, almost losing my house, losing my figure, and losing all elasticity in my facial skin. Then there are the biggies. I've suffered the loss of family members (human and canine) who are dear to me. I've suffered the sight of my children's faces when they are sick. I've suffered with the struggle to understand why I can't help all the homeless people standing at the traffic light in the cold. The ones that have no winter coat. I've suffered with cancer and a bladder disease.

See that? I did it. I made you feel guilty. I did it while I was suffering. We're good at it, I tell ya! So you still don't get it? You still don't understand why you owe my husband the note? It's because every single day I'm able to wake up, feel my aches, pains, and emotional distress, and still go out and face the world. It's because when I do face the world, I face it with a smile and a gentleness in my heart. It's because you don't have to hear me complain about how my pee stings, my hands won't grasp, my pain is throbbing, and my emotional state is digressing. That's what my husband is for.

He told me to say "you're welcome".

Chapter Four: Can't Get What I Want, Can't Give What I Want

Part of the zoo.

So now that I'm all grown up, and I somehow didn't kill my kids before they could grow up, I find myself an empty nester (except for the dogs - three now, and the damn bird - more on him later) waiting for weddings and grandchildren. I find myself trying to please all people, even myself. I find myself doing a lot of reflection and hoping that I taught the kids all the right things.   Did I teach them love, honor, and respect for both themselves and others? Did I teach them how to balance work and family? Did I teach them how to enjoy the things they've earned yet not to forget that others haven't had the privileges that they have? And of course, and most importantly, did I teach them to love me enough so that one day when I repeat myself due to Alzheimer's, can't wipe my own butt due to arthritis, and can't stand since I've fallen and can't get up, they'll be there to listen, wipe, pick me up, and fill my glass with prune juice until it overflows?

Sad Birthday

Yesterday, was my husband's birthday. Because of it, today we are both very sad. To understand why, I have to take you back to 1999. We were living in Texas with two little girls, and we were days away from moving across the country to Connecticut when our nanny walked in for her last day of work with us. But she didn't walk in empty handed. She walked in with an eight-week-old puppy. Now in a normal household with two children, a puppy coming through the door would be followed my pleas from the children asking if they could keep it. Our household, was uber normal. What I mean to say is that I did not have only two little girls. I also had a little husband, two other dogs, three birds, two ninety-gallon fish tanks, and an untold number of hamsters. I could clearly hear the pleas from the girls. The pleas from hubby were even louder. To this day, I could swear the other two dogs chimed in telling me they were in need of a new brother too. The little husband was flying ahead the next day. Me, mama bear, would be leaving with the clan by car a few days afterward. The pleas continued right up until I completely gave in, and said we could throw the puppy in the car with everyone else as we drove up to Connecticut. (Please don't fret, I did leave the two fish tanks behind).

Before I knew what hit me, I found myself in a teeny tiny rental house with the whole motley crew. In the past, I was always the grown up in the family when it came to getting the animals to the vet, the groomers, and making sure they were properly trained. But training the puppy was all too much for me to deal with among the boxes that needed unpacking, the children that needed school registering, and all the other minutia of a move. As the saying goes, the shit really hit the fan when I came home one rainy day to find the puppy shaking the mud off of himself and onto the wall of the rental while observing the newly chewed up outlet on said wall. New puppy, had to go. I found a lovely family who had recently lost one of their two dogs and desperately needed a companion for the one still alive. I felt relief that I had lifted the burden off myself by finding the puppy a fitting new home. My girls are now thirty and thirty-one-years old, and I'm still the bad guy. My husband is now fifty-seven, and I'm still the bad guy.

Over the years we enjoyed the pleasures of the two dogs we brought with us and mourned their loss. We've had new ones come to share our lives with us. As is tradition in our household, we still have two dogs that grace us with warm welcomes every time we come home. But here's where the sad birthday comes in. Our furry friends have always been mutts from whatever local shelter we could find. My husband grew up with a golden retriever by his side. He's always wanted another one. He's an uncomplicated man with very simple desires. He never wants anything for his birthday other than the warmth of his loved ones around him. For weeks before his birthday, I stressed over what I could give him that would really mean something to him. All I could think of was a golden retriever. For the holidays this year, the girls gave him the name of one they paid to sponsor in his name. Clearly, I knew that the single thing in the world that would make my husband happy for his birthday would be to give him a golden retriever.

I tried. I tried with all my might to accept the fact that we would finally have to have three dogs, and I would be raising another puppy. My dear husband has given me everything I ever wanted. He wanted only one thing: a golden retriever. I sit here ashamed to say that I just couldn't do it. I just couldn't give him the one thing he truly wants in life. So here we are, both sad the day after his birthday - me because I was incapable of giving the love of my life the only meaningful thing that would make him happy and him because he didn't receive it.

The good news is that birthdays come around every year. The bad news is that I'll have to struggle with this again next year.

The following year, of course, did come. I broke down. We now own a golden retriever. I can officially say that three dogs, a saltwater reef tank, and a thirty-three-year-old cockatoo are a sufficient zoo for me, and that's not even counting the mice we get every year in the basement!

Lessons In Hatred: Is Your Congressman as Smart as a Third-Grader?

Many years ago, I learned about **Jane Elliott***, a teacher who, in 1968, tried to teach her students a lesson in bigotry by segregating her class by eye color. Elliott posed a question to her third-grade students: did they know how it would feel to be judged by the color of their skin? They weren't quite sure how to answer. She suggested that they wouldn't know how it felt unless they'd gone through it, so she singled out all of the blue-eyed students in the class from all of the brown-eyed students.

She told her students that the blue-eyed people were better and smarter than brown-eyed people. "This is a fact," she said. She told the brown-eyed students that they had to stay in from recess, and couldn't drink from the water fountain or play with the blue-eyed children, because they weren't as good.

After only a few minutes, when the teacher was looking for her yard stick, one of the blue-eyed students suggested she might need it for brown-eyed people who got out of hand. A physical fight broke out among the students that day caused by a blue-eyed child teasing a brown-eyed child for no other reason than he had brown eyes.

The following day, Ms. Elliott reversed the roles. She explained to the students that she had been wrong the day before — that actually it was the brown-eyed children who were better than the blue-eyed children.

On the third day, the teacher questioned the children about how they felt about the previous two days. One student said that "it seemed like when we were down on the bottom, everything bad was happening to us." Another stated that "the way we were treated, it felt like you didn't even want to try to do anything."

Ms. Elliott herself said that she "watched what had been marvellous, cooperative, wonderful, thoughtful children, turn into nasty, vicious, discriminating little third graders in the space of 15 minutes."

It took only 15 minutes!

The teacher said that even their daily flash card exercises were affected by the experiment: On both days, the "superior" students worked with their flash cards in half the time they normally did.

I've often thought about Mrs. Elliott's experiment with racism over the years. I've wondered if things have changed. Evidence indicates that they have not.

I wouldn't say that it shocks me, but I will say that it scares me. A series of experiments in which very young children were asked to choose between two dolls (one black and one white) or among five images of children of various skin tones revealed some harsh truths.

"Which doll is the nice doll?"

"Which doll looks bad?"

"Which is the good one?"

"Which is the smart one?"

The children being interviewed were black, Latino, and white. Time and again the children identified the black child or the darkest child negatively. When asked why they gave the answers they did, the children gave some of the following responses:

Asked "Which doll is pretty?" an African-American boy who pointed to the white doll said, "Because she's white."

Asked "Which doll is nice?" another African-American boy who pointed at the white doll said, "Because she's white."

Asked "Which doll is smart?" a white girl pointed to the white doll. Asked why, she said, "Because she looks like me."

It made me so sad, but I was OK until this one brought the first tear to my eye: Asked which skin color she liked, an African-American girl pointed to a picture of a white doll. When asked why, *she pointed to her own skin* and said, "I don't like the way brown looks, 'cause brown looks really nasty for some reason."

When a Hispanic boy pointed to a white doll when asked "Which doll is good?" I could not hold back the tears. His reason: "Because I'm not scared of whiter people. Because I trust them more. But others, like this other one," — indicating the black doll — "I don't trust them as much."

We need Jane Elliott back!

After the horrors of Charlottesville, Virginia in August of 2017 and after hearing these young children's opinions, what's in store for future generations?

It was only twenty-five years after a Central Park jogger was beaten and murdered, that the "Central Park Five" settled a $40 million lawsuit for wrongfully being convicted of that crime. It took third graders 15 minutes to learn a lesson in hatred. It took the entire justice system twenty-five years to correct their misguided assumption of five youths.

I wonder, what will our nation be like 25 years from now? What could Mrs. Elliott's lessons teach to our Congressmen?

My country is being split into extremes. I no longer see respect between the political parties. Each side digs their heels into the soil and shows hatred to the opposing side. I find this hard to comprehend. I have yet to meet another human being who agrees with me on every topic, on every level, in every aspect of my life. Does this mean I can't have a discussion with someone, disagree, and then go share a drink and a laugh together?

How about if we force the blue-eyed Democrats and the blue-eyed Republicans into a room where they can hear all of the political discussion and debate among their colleagues, but they are not allowed to speak in any way. They have to sit for days and hear pro-life opinions and pro-choice opinions, but they are never allowed to voice their own opinions-not even to their blue-eyed colleagues. They must observe their brown-, black-, green-, and grey-eyed Congressmen scream out their opinions on gun control, same-sex marriage, the legalization of marijuana, and health care.

Perhaps after several weeks of this torture, the blue-eyed Congressmen will observe that, while they have been forced to listen to the debate, unable to voice an opinion of their own, unable to secure the backing of other like-minded individuals, they actually heard the speakers for the very first time-even the ones with whom they disagree. Maybe, just maybe, they will realize that nothing is being accomplished because no one else is listening.

Maybe, when they are finally allowed to rejoin their non-blue-eyed colleagues, they can tell them about how much hatred they witnessed while they were unable to participate. If these ostracized Congressmen could learn the same lessons as Mrs. Elliott's third-grade students, I wonder if they might actually respect each other enough to consider the unthinkable: compromise.

Then all Americans could applaud them and be proud to live in the world's largest cultural melting pot - one that contains people who look different and think differently, and people who respect one another enough to listen to each other, make laws with each other, and live harmoniously in the greatest country on Earth.

To my great honor, Jane Elliott actually saw this published essay and wrote to me thanking me for its contents. Although I've not yet had the opportunity to meet her in person, we have exchanged correspondence. It is my privilege to call her my friend.

Answering Life's Questions

Should I sock away money for retirement? Should I stay on my diet? Should I exercise? Should I take the vacation? Should I buy the dream house?

These are the questions I ask myself as I go through my daily life. I'm always wondering if I should err on the side of caution and save money for a rainy day, retirement, or even a sunny day. I wonder if passing up that piece of chocolate cake was really a good idea. Was I being prudent by keeping my calorie count down, or should I enjoy myself when the opportunity presents itself? I'm one of the lucky ones. I don't actually hate exercise. I enjoy a good swim or a nice long walk. But I can't say that I crave lifting weights to keep my bones and muscles from deteriorating, or that I enjoy a good huff, puff, and sweat just for fun. Should I blow off the workout and meet a friend for deep dish pizza, or am I better off in the long run by going ahead with the sweat and pain, and opting for the salad with the dressing on the side while passing up oozing cheese and melty crust?

Well I'm here to tell ya that I've come up with total and complete solution to my problem: my death date. Now hear me out. I don't think it's the least bit morbid. Actually, I think it would be quite liberating. Just think how sad it would be if you heard that I died, and my last meal was cottage cheese and a celery stick. Had I only known that I had one more day to live, believe me, it would not be a day filled with "Sweatin' to the Oldies" and eating little more than a lettuce leaf. I'd be spending every penny on whatever made me happy and eating every last delicious favorite food I could get my hands on. Now before you call me shallow. I didn't say what I'd spend the money on. Perhaps I'd spend it on fine dining in the company of all my loved ones. Perhaps I'd enjoy donating some of it to experience the joy of seeing it put to good use. But the bottom line is that if I knew my death date, it would answer all of my burning questions.

For instance, if I knew that I was going to live into my nineties or beyond, I'd know I needed to squirrel away a lot of savings so that I could live comfortably in my old age. If I knew that I was going to live to a ripe old age, I'd eat healthfully and exercise with the plan to live those years well. If I knew that cutting out sugar and flour would cause me to live that older healthier life, I'd cut them out in a heart beat...to keep my heart, well... beating. If I knew I had many years ahead to take one trip a year to see all the sites I hope to see, I'd pace myself. If I knew I had plenty of time to buy my dream home and years ahead to enjoy it, I'd penny pinch 'til the cows came home...or at least the dogs, from their sunbathing in the back yard.

Yet, if I knew I had only a short time left on this Earth, I can tell you, without a shadow of a doubt, that saving money, dieting, and exercising would not be on my priority list. Flour and sugar would be at the top of the food pyramid, that dream home that I've been saving for would never be built, and the savings never accrued as I would spend that money on the here and now with those I cherish.

Now you might say that I should be living for the here and now anyway. I should be spending my time with those whom I love and spending my money on the things I believe are important. You would not be wrong in saying this. But honestly, if you knew you had only a short time to live, wouldn't you do things differently? And if you knew without a shadow of a doubt that you had a long life expectancy, wouldn't that too change your perspective?

Yep, I want my death date. I want to know that if tomorrow is my last day on Earth, I didn't spend it paying the bills, after a spin class that made every muscle in my body ache, and eating grass. Because let's face it, since we don't know our death date, we have to play the odds. The bills have to get paid, the savings have to be put away. And were I to eat all my favorite foods without ever passing one up, I'd be as fat as a cow and encouraging death to come too soon.

Let's hear it for having death dates divulged. You can opt in or opt out. If you want to go through life as you always have, without the knowledge of your final day, you can have that option. But if you do want to know, you can be like me, and be happy in the knowledge that your last day on earth will be spent surrounded by the people you wish to be surrounded by and with anything in your belly that isn't green or healthy.

There would be one other awesome benefit to knowing your death date: guilt-free living. Of course, I think this is only a benefit if you know your death date is coming soon, but nonetheless, it would be the first time ever you could spend, and eat, and play hooky without a guilty bone in your body. How awesome would that be?

But alas, I have no means of obtaining my actual death date, so for the time being, I say play the odds. Do a little of both. Do the saving, do the dieting, do the exercising, but don't forget to spend a little for enjoyment now with those you love, eat the things you love but in moderation, move enough to be healthy by trying to find exercises you can actually enjoy, and try, try, to make each day count. After all, tomorrow may be your death date.

As The Tables Turn

When I call my mom, every other day, her first response to me is almost always "well hello stranger." You'd think I never call her. If I called her every single day, she'd respond the same way. If I called her twice a day, I'd hear the same.

So it goes without saying that when my grown daughters call me, I try very hard to simply say hello and not add a side dish of guilt to their plates. But I can't help but elevate my voice with excitement when one of them is on the other end of the line. I can't help but get excited when they come to visit. I wait all week for a sighting; I clean house, cook their favorite meal, and clear my calendar, all for a two or three-hour visit with them. When they leave to return to their lives, I never feel like I've had enough of them. They bring their significant others and their laundry, and I welcome both with equal enthusiasm.

They know I love them, but they don't quite understand my extreme enthusiasm when they tell me they want to come over for a visit even if it's just to pick up the suitcase they want to borrow. I should write a soap opera and call it *As The Tables Turn,* because one day, they will have children of their own. I expect by then, there will be an episode in which they call one of their children to ask when they can get together and the response they hear will be "Aww Mom, I just sent my drone out to you last week, what more do you want?"

<u>Chapter Five: Loss and Love</u>

What do a Lincoln Town Car and a jar of mustard have in common?

I have had the fortune of losing very few loved ones to death in my life. My grandparents have all perished, but I still enjoy the healthy company of both of my parents, my brother, my sisters-in-law and brothers-in-law, my children, and of course, my Marty. Unfortunately, Marty's parents have both passed. I never had the honor of knowing his dad well. I did have the privilege of knowing his mother until her recent passing at age ninety-one. This first essay was written only three days before she died. The second, was written while I was still in mourning. The last one, is more recent. I had to live more life before I could understand that I needed to do more walking in other people's shoes to understand other people's pain and not just my own.

It had been another one of those glass pretty-darn-empty times. I had had the cancer back to back several times within a two-year span and ended up with yet a new diagnosis for an unrelated bladder disease. So, of course, I found myself in the hospital for the bladder thing trying to get discharged because I was supposed to have another cancer surgery scheduled at an entirely different hospital the next day. When mom came to visit me in my hospital room, well, to say the least, I'm not sure how Marty and I handled one more thing.

Mom, however, handled it with the same grace and dignity that she'd handled everything else in her life. I thank her, for leaving me her son.

In Case Tissues

She came for me. She pulled into the parking lot that day in her forest green Lincoln Town car. It was huge - almost as big as her life has been. I remember riding in it on that front bench seat that always had a box of tissues resting in the middle - just "in case." At 87, she barely even used her cane. It seemed like more of a security blanket than anything. Maybe it made her feel that she looked the part of stoic matriarch. She didn't need it. I already knew. She walked in the room in her matter-of-fact manner. Her skirt covered her knees but not her calves. She always had nice legs, and she knew it. She had on her signature scarf tied around her neck to hide the wrinkles that had taunted her for decades. Those were the wrinkles we fought about. It's the only time I ever remember disagreeing with her in all of our years together.

The fight had been the week before. I accompanied her to the cosmetic surgeon's office so she could discuss her impending face lift. She wanted to prove to me he was qualified and hoped I would agree with her assessment. I did not. Always a strong willed woman, she booked the surgery anyway. I was so upset with her that I wouldn't even join her for lunch after the appointment - a decision I've regretted for many years now. That day, she stopped taking her daily aspirin in preparation of the surgery.

But on this day, a week after the incident, she was coming to see me in my hospital bed. I could see the love she had for me reflecting back through her thick round glasses. The reflection was like a Vermeer painting - her, big as life itself, and me, the tiny reflection staring back in glaring detail. Her compassion radiated from the light in her eyes, through those thick frames, as it lit up the walls of that dreary room. The ambient light surrounded her as she sat to converse with me until she bowed her head as if someone had switched off the light.

I called out to her but there was no response. I could see my reflection and the light oozing its way out of her. It seemed to seep down the hall, through the doors, and into the parking lot where it punctured the tires of the Town Car causing a slow, quiet release of air until they were flat.

I pushed my call button. I screamed into the speaker that I needed help immediately. "It's not me," I said. "It's my mother-in-law. She's having a stroke!" They sent in a nurse as Mom's head lifted. It was like watching a slow motion movie rewind. First her head eased its way back to the erect position. Then I saw the tires inflate, the slow ooze of the light holding my reflection, the light switched back on, and the ambient glow reappeared. The nurse said mom was fine and headed out the door. I screamed at her and told her that she was not fine and insisted on seeing a doctor at once. In a moment, the half a dozen doctors making their rounds entered my room. Mom insisted she was fine. These feckless doctors insisted she was fine. I insisted she was not fine. They had her stand and walk across the room, tell them her name and the day's date. She performed all with precision. They said they would stop back by in twenty minutes or so when they completed their rounds. The word "no" came out of my mouth from somewhere deep in my gut. It shot out with a point that was sharp, and loud, and clear. I pointed it at the group of doctors, stabbed them with it, and then rotated it clockwise right into their guts. It didn't work. They turned to leave the room. As they did, one of them must have switched off the light, because it was happening again. "Look at her now! Ask her your questions now!" One of them reluctantly turned back toward her only to see her head once again bowing down to the ground that swept away the reflection, but this time, he saw it too. They asked her to stand, but the cane, still useless, laid on the floor in a puddle next to the light and the reflection. She collapsed in their arms.

I suppose if you're going to have a stroke, the hospital is the best place to have one. My husband called to tell me he was on the way to come see me. I told him to come faster. We called his four siblings and within hours, the whole family was there to support our matriarch in every way she had always supported us.

She survived the stroke, and after months of rehab, we managed to get her home. She lost a lot that day - the day of her stroke. But she didn't lose her position as stoic matriarch. Her body may have failed her, but her mind was still intact. She could bring up memories the rest of us had long forgotten.

Although no longer independent years, the following three and a half years were good ones for her. She celebrated her 90th birthday with two huge parties, saw the birth of her first three great-grandchildren, the marriage of two of her grandchildren, and the engagement of another. We all regularly visited her and shared in her company whenever she had the energy, and she always kept her sense of humor about her. When we would ask why she was always so tired, she would tell us we would be too if we had breathed in and out for ninety years. I can't say that time since her stroke was all good. She struggled with her religious faith for the first time in her life, she was in and out of the hospital for various ailments on numerous occasions, and she often forgot if she last saw you yesterday or last week. Her short term memory was clouded. Her long term memory was intact. But in the big picture, I've been honored to still know her and share life events with her.

I called her "Mom" from the start. When she held my babies in her arms, they were her babies too. When my father-in-law passed away, I held those arms wrapping mine around them as she had wrapped hers around my babies. When the cancer came, she watched over me. When Sandy came, and she lost power, I drove an hour and a half to retrieve her and drive her back to my house. I made her stay in the warmth of our home. It got warmer before she left.

But last December hit me, and the rest of our family hard. She fell and broke her hip. There we all were, rallied around the hospital waiting room waiting for word post-surgery. The results this time were not so good. She has barely gained consciousness since the surgery. We tried medications, nourishment, therapies, and finally got her back home so she could be comfortable in her own surroundings. She turned ninety-one last week. We didn't have a party.

Where did my mother-in-law go? Where is the woman who raised my husband - the one who taught him of integrity and compassion by setting her own example?

I want to take her out to lunch, the one I declined. I want to take her for her face lift, the one I was too stubborn to agree with. What I don't want, is to use the "in case" tissues from the front seat of her Lincoln Town car.

The Echo of the Youngest Son

My mother-in-law passed away last week just a few days after her 91st birthday. She is survived by her five children, eleven grandchildren, and now nine great-grandchildren. She left all of us with amazing gifts of love, respect, honor, and grace. She left me with the most precious gift of all: her youngest son.

Mom always said two things about my husband. She said that his nickname should be "Horizontal" because that was the position he was most frequently in, and that if he had been the first child, he would have been the only child. Both statements are completely true. I wonder however, if she actually knew just how true they were.

When we met, it was love at first sight. I didn't believe you could possibly truly love someone after only laying eyes on them. But then it happened to me. I became a believer.

I was a southern girl visiting New York on a cold snowy February day. It was on the campus of Cornell University in Ithaca. I went to see the school to consider transferring there. A mutual friend introduced us. We spent a few hours together playing cards with her and one of his other friends. We just kept locking eyes. Eventually, we decided to join another group to go to dinner and a hockey game. As we walked to the Pizzeria, he saw my top coat button unbuttoned and my hat string untied. He took it upon himself to button and tie me to assure my warmth with the utmost of care and concern. After only one day of knowing one another, I flew back to Texas. He called his mom to tell her he met the girl he was going to marry.

We've had thirty-four years of life together. One of my first life lessons from my husband came in our first year of marriage. He was a graduate student and home most of the day. I was working to support us. I came home after a hard day to find him sacked out on the couch with his head covered in pillows and a pile of dishes in the kitchen sink. I went ballistic. I ranted about how I'd worked all day only to come home to a stack of dirty dishes. With one eyeball poking out from the mound of pillows, he calmly looked at me with a loving smile, welcomed me home, rolled his head back where it had been, and went back to sleep. It was later that I found out he'd had friends over earlier in the day. They'd made a mess everywhere. When he checked the clock to see I'd be home soon, he collected the mess placing everything in the sink where he believed it all lived. I tried to pick a fight. He tried to make me happy.

When I anxiously left our newborn home alone with him for one of the first times, I came home once again to find my husband sacked out on the couch. This time, in addition to the pillows covering his face, the baby was sprawled out on his belly and sobbing into his chest. When I hysterically questioned how he could possibly sleep while the baby was crying her eyes out, he explained to me that she was calmer now after she'd had a difficult poop. He smiled as he described it by likening it to the contents of a fine jar of Grey Poupon. Ya gotta love a guy who admires poop.

These are the stories of my husband on "stop" mode, when his mind relaxes and he's horizontal. He also has "go" mode. His mind works as fast as an Intel Core i7 processor (and yes, I had to look that up). He invented ADD before it was fashionable.

When I fought hard to kick my narcotic drug addiction after years of cancer, I was easily frustrated with him. He was watching a ball game, surfing the net, and making phone calls. "Why was I not receiving his undivided attention?" I thought. But if he had turned off that game, I would have panicked in the deafening silence. He was surfing the net to find any and all suggestions on easing my withdrawal. He was calling doctors, clinics, and family members to find out how best to help me. He missed weeks of work risking the stability of his job, all to sit by my side.

And don't forget that whole Super Storm Sandy story and how he actually thanked me for doing what I would have done anyway. He said, "thank you." What on earth did he have to thank me for? He was thanking me for taking care of his mom, whom I had always loved, and he was thanking me for taking care of the house we could no longer own.

But it was I who should have been doing the thanking. It was I who should have thanked him for the lesson of the dishes in the sink. His thoughtfulness outweighed my anger. It was I who should have thanked him for being so calm with our first born who surely would not have ended up as such an amazing adult if I alone had raised her. It was I who should have thanked him for watching over my mangled, addicted body as he nursed me back to health while juggling so many other tasks at once all on my behalf. And it was I who should thank his mother for raising him - the boy she called "Horizontal" - the boy who she said would have been an only child had he been her first born instead of her last.

I cannot mourn the death of my mother-in-law. I cannot mourn her loss because I cannot mourn that which has not been lost. Her strength of love, respect, honor, and grace have not been lost upon her death. They live on in all her children, but you can hear them the loudest when they echo back from the heartbeats of her youngest son.

Take a Walk in My Shoes

Put your shoes on and come take a walk with me, a nice brisk walk on a cold winter's day. We'll walk and we'll talk for three or four miles. Put your shoes on, and you'll see how healthy and vibrant I am. Put your shoes on and listen to me tell you all about my joys of the past week since we last walked together. I'll tell you how I heard my husband laugh, and how it made my heart warm despite the cold outside air. I'll tell you how excited I was when one of my essays was accepted for publication. I'll tell you how I ate a half gallon of ice cream in twenty-four hours on my new diet, but ate steamed broccoli and broiled skinless chicken for dinner so my husband could see how strict I'm being on my new health conscious plan.

Put your shoes on and I'll listen to you as we walk. I want to hear about what's going on in your life. I want to encourage you to keep walking with me so we can both stay healthy. Put your shoes on. Let's take a walk so I can hear about how your week went. I want to know what warmed your heart this week, what got you excited, and even what mistakes you made. I want to help you fix your problems and share in your joy.

Now put my shoes on. Walk just one of those miles in them. See just how they feel. You notice that when I stop talking and listen to you, I listen with great concentration and consideration, but with great pain. You notice the pain in my mouth from decades of recurrent tongue cancer. You notice the sharp pinch in my hip from my herniated disc. Put on my shoes, and you'll see that I haven't always had the material things I now have. You'll see how grateful I am for what I have and how unimportant most of these things are to me. Put on my shoes, and you'll see what is important to me: our friendship, the love of my family, my health and yours. Put on my shoes and you can see the serious side of my almost lifelong struggle with cancer. Put on my shoes and see how many times I've been taken advantage of in business and in my naiveté. I'd like to take a walk in your shoes as well. No matter how hard I try, unless I wear your shoes, I will never completely understand you. I will never completely know you.

But there are a few things I do know. I know how much wiser I am if I only try to make yours fit, my neighbor's fit, the grocery clerk's fit. I know how much happier I am walking in my own shoes today than the one's I wore in my twenties, and I know that when I get burned in business or in life, I just need to lace up a new pair and step out of the sun.

If I always stay outside in the brisk winter's cold, I'll never stay warm. If I always stay outside, I won't know what I missed. I'll grow old with regrets of what I missed - what could have been. And if I never at least try to walk in another man's shoes, at least try to make them fit, I will never know what I don't know. I'll never know if it was worth it. At this time in my life, I'm up for a challenge. I'd like to walk in as many pairs of other people's shoes as possible. May I start with yours?

A Touched Life

What would you do if you received the following note written on a yellow Post It note in a handwritten scrawl?

"Good Morning, I like you! You are down to EARTH!...I am down to EARTH good person. Please is it ok if I call you sometime? or we can go to lunch...? My number is 000-000-0000."

If I'd seen this note out of context, I would have thought it was written by a school age child. It looked like one of those sixth grade notes that boys wrote back when they were still innocent and stricken by puppy love. You know the kind...

"I like you. If you like me too check

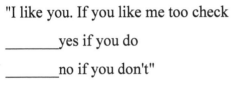

_____yes if you do

_____no if you don't"

Remember those? If you're a girl with any compassion at all, even at that age, these notes could really put you on the spot. If you said yes, it meant you liked the boy. You checked yes, and you were now going "steady." If you didn't like the boy, you had a dilemma on your hands. To say no meant rejection, but to say yes when you didn't really mean it forced you into a whole new set of circumstances you preferred to stay away from.

Once when I was in junior high, I knew a boy with a crush on me. I tried everything to dissuade him, but to no avail. No matter what I did, short of being completely blunt and totally rude, I could not get him to leave me alone. To make matters worse, he was sweet. I missed several weeks of school due to a bout with mono. He was the only one to come to my house to bring me get well gifts. What's a girl to do when she just doesn't reciprocate a boy's feelings? Eventually, the whole thing petered out as things fortunately do when you're in junior high, and he moved on to the next victim...err...girl. I can't say that I even remember his name.

By the time I got to college, I hadn't grown any wiser. There was a boy in my freshman science lab that would follow me every day after class attempting to carry on a conversation with me. It's not that I had a boyfriend at the time. It's just that I found this guy to be rather creepy. He didn't travel among my circle of friends, and he just plain gave me the heebie-jeebies. Just as I'd done back in junior high, I tried to be aloof, acted disinterested, scooted out of class in a hurry, anything to escape a confrontation. But then his desperation kicked in and the following line came out of his mouth:

"Do you think that sometime between now and the end of the year, you could find a time to go out with me?"

OMG, how do you answer that one? "Nope, sorry, I have plans every day for the next 365 days?" "Sorry, I lead an extremely tight schedule?" Honestly, how do you say no to that one without totally deflating the guy? Unlike junior high, these things don't just melt away in a day like snow in the sun. Somehow, I managed to scoot away as if in a terrible hurry, told him I was so sorry, but I had to go, and that I'd see him in lab the next day. But low and behold, the guy was actually stalking me. At the time, I was playing intramural co-ed softball right after that class. The guy followed me there! I went into shock when I spotted him across the softball field. I quickly explained my dilemma to a male friend on the team, and without a moment's hesitation, he went into action, putting his arm around me, and giving me a tight snuggle. By the time stalker dude made his way up to the bleachers, I introduced him to my "boyfriend," and it was quite clear to him that I was taken.

Ok, I'm guilty of lying, and putting on a false front, but I couldn't think of a kinder way to let this guy down. He hadn't done anything to me other than to admire me. I just couldn't see hurting his feelings, and I certainly couldn't see going out with him. Problem solved.

Now that I'm a happily married woman, it seems quite easy to me to avoid even potential male interest when I put out a regular "I'm happily married" vibe. Post marriage, I don't recall ever really having much of a problem with men. Now, my issues have been transferred to women.

A few years back, some of my gal pals and I put together a regular game night. Once in a while, we were short by a girl, so I decided to add one or two friends to the list as alternates. I received an e-mail from one of the regulars stating that she thought we'd have to cancel game night due to being short a fourth player. I shot her an e-mail back telling her it was no problem and that I'd invited another friend to fill in so the game could go on as planned. I'll never forget how stunned I was when I received a response back from her telling me that she didn't want any new friends.

She didn't have time for any new friends, and she didn't want to be forced into making a new friend. I was speechless. Who doesn't need friends? Besides, what was the big deal? It was one night. It was supposed to be "game" night - a fun event. Although, I certainly felt she would need to be cordial to our alternate player, there was no law that said that she then had to entertain a lifelong friendship with the girl. I don't do girl drama well, so in the end, I lied to both of them. I told the regular that the alternate couldn't play after all, and I told the alternate that even with her, we just didn't have enough to make the game that night. This happened several years ago, but I can still feel the back of my hand wiping the sweat from my brow as I dodged that bullet.

So imagine my reaction, when I received the note...the yellow sticky note that said "I like you," and "will you be my friend?" To put it all in context, the note was from a temp who was filling in at my then-office. We had a tiny little office of reporters who came in, logged on, typed for eight hours, and then went home. It was truly the least social office I've ever worked in. For me though, it worked out just fine. I only worked there part-time, and had an outside social life I was quite happy with.

This woman, we'll call her Catherine, started filling in for us as a temp about two weeks after one of our reporters quit. I soon learned that I was the only one who said hello and good morning to Catherine when she came in or when we passed in the kitchen to grab a quick coffee. Suddenly, with tear-filled eyes, she came to my desk, handed me the note, and stood there waiting for a reply. My immediate reaction was to stand up and give her a hug, which is exactly what I did. But where do you go from there? How can one possibly answer the question "can I call you sometime," by saying no? How cruel would that be? I looked her in her teary eyes and said "yes, of course," and she went back to her desk and to work. I tried to go back to mine.

I sat there dumfounded as I read the note again. "I am down to EARTH good person. Please is it ok if I call you sometime?" This note really threw me for a loop. I felt so badly for Catherine. She appeared to be a woman in her mid to late sixties. She'd mentioned to me the previous day in the office kitchen that she had lived in our area for seven years and still felt like she had just moved here. I had lived here for two and felt all settled in. I had my circle of friends, lots of family, and a full, nicely rounded life. Was I becoming my regular game night friend? Was I too busy and self-involved to allow a new person into my life? Would I tell another lie to get out of this?

All I could think of was a story I remember hearing, about how one life can so easily touch another. I remember hearing about a boy who became a high school valedictorian and gave a commencement speech honoring his best friend. It was the story of the day the two of them met. He said that was the same day he planned on killing himself. It wasn't until that speech that the friend knew how much that one interaction changed his friend's life.

How could I turn away this woman's tear-stained desperate face?

Within a few moments of the whole encounter, my boss told Catherine to go home. He said that we didn't need her anymore that day, but to come in the next day, Friday. I didn't work there on Fridays, so I feared I wouldn't see her again. I shot out a text to a friend, Lisa, who had just recently complained that she had too much time on her hands now that she was working only part-time, and that she didn't have anyone to go do things with. I told her I wanted her to meet Catherine. She stopped by at lunch time the following Monday.

When I texted Catherine to tell her all about Lisa, and that we had a lunch date with her on Monday, this was her response back to me:

"Thank you so much! Hopefully we can do more in the future! I am so happy, I pray that we will remain friends like my friends back home for the rest of our lives. Take care, have a nice evening!"

I'm not quite sure what I'm in for here, but I'm done telling little lies. Perhaps, just maybe, there's a life that's been touched here. Perhaps it's mine.

<u>Chapter Six: Life's Musings</u>

Ya'll	Ya'll  is a real word!

In 1980 it ain't a real word, but the 2017 dictionary tells a different story!

Gee whiz, I've made it through being ashamed of myself, surviving 9/11 with Marty, and surviving cancer a gazillion times. All this survival makes that glass of mine half full again. Yes, I did say half "full." I did survive them all, didn't I? Being the selfish type that I am though, I wanted to see it completely full again. But I keep dwelling on silly things like being a lady in waiting. Yep, that's me. I'm a lady in waiting. I'm waiting for one of my daughters to get married to her fiancé and the other to get engaged. I'm waiting to attend the weddings. And for heavens' sake, I want to be a grandma preferably before my death date! So now I find myself rolling other ideas around in my head. I roll them around so that I force myself to live in the present. I don't want to keep being the lady in waiting. Don't get me wrong, I can hardly wait until I see my girls happily married, with children and happy lives of their own. But in the meantime, I need to keep appreciating what I have and filling up my glass. So I think about things I have in abundance. I think about the love I have in my marriage. I think about the love I have for those girls of mine. I think about the love I have for my parents and siblings, and my glass just keeps spilling over.

But I also think about weird day-to-day things. I think about myself and my fellow Americans and the abundance of physical stuff that we accumulate. I think about what I hope my grandkids will be named (even though, I'll have no choice in the matter). I think about things when I'm standing in line at the grocery store, washing my hands in the bathroom, and what an awesome president I'd make if I only I would just run for office in 2020. Don't judge. I know you think about this stuff too. You think about stuff when you're driving, you think about stuff when you're showering, and you think about stuff when you're trying to fall asleep. I'm the only one crazy enough to divulge what I'm thinking, but I do admit it; I have to divulge these things. Otherwise, they'll just keep rolling around in my brain and I'll never get to sleep.

Thanks for helping me sleep well tonight.

Stuff

I recently became a renter for the first time in almost thirty years. Shortly after moving into the rental, I had the misfortune of assisting my family in dismantling my mother-in-law's home after her death. I came to the conclusion that in actuality, we are all renters. I don't care if you have a mortgage, own your home outright, or pay a landlord. In the scheme of life, eventually we all die, and someone has to go throw out our stuff, which we no longer own because we are dead. Thus, we were actually only renting it during life.

Now that I have come to this conclusion, I'm trying to figure out why we are all hoarders. Since we're renting all of our stuff anyway, and eventually have to give it back, why do we need so much of it, and what are we doing with it all?

In the early twentieth century a typical home in America was about 700 to 1200 square feet. Entire families lived within the confines of this space. Today, the average home is 2,000 square feet or more. It's not uncommon for one or two people to be living in the entire house. Somehow, we feel we have to stuff our houses with...well...stuff. It starts out as decorating. First we need a new couch, a coffee table, and a bedroom set. Then we need the appliances: TV, lawn mower, washer and dryer, mix master, blender. Then we need the gadgets: can openers, bread makers, ice cream makers, slicers, dicers, choppers, sealers. Before ya know it we need our toys too: bikes, scrapbooking supplies, wood working tools, jewelry making, sewing, skiing, surfing. The list goes on.

And now, we've created an entire industry just for our stuff. There are businesses built around accumulating it, and businesses built around getting rid of it. Suddenly, we started seeing public storage units. We had so much stuff, we were bursting at the seams and needed not only the bigger house, but an extra place to keep our junk. God forbid we ever part with any of it. This, of course, is all stuff that we *need*. So we start to pay a monthly fee to keep our stuff in day care. Why not, there's child day care, doggy day care, why not stuff day care? But then the guilt sets in. Poor stuff, we haven't visited it enough. Perhaps we should plan the next vacation to the public storage facility so that we can spend time visiting our stuff. After all, we might love some of our stuff more than we love some of our family members, and we make a point of visiting them don't we? But in actuality, we rarely visit our stuff, if at all. We just continue to rent a storage unit month after month to keep a bunch of stuff we don't ever use. We've created a mass of entrepreneurs to help us with our stuff. Stores have opened up that sell only things to store our stuff. New experts have arrived on the scene known as professional organizers who can help us figure out where to put it all. We even have therapists who have become experts on hoarding and can treat us with regular sessions to help us with our illness.

After we've finished collecting all we think we can handle, then we find we are in need of the massive purge. After lifetimes of hoarding stuff, the kids move out of the house, and we finally decide to downsize. Now enter the other half of the business end of Americans and their stuff. What to toss? What to keep? There are experts we can hire to help us with that too. There are even entire companies solely devoted to hauling away all that stuff it took us decades to accumulate.

But now I worry. I have a serious concern for the future of our stuff. You see in this digital age, not only are new businesses popping up to help us store all our digital junk, but they tell me that once you put something out there into cyberspace, it's there forever...no take backs. So eventually, aren't we going to use up all that cyber space? Where will we go from there? Has anybody thought of that? Perhaps since we've found no life on the moon, we should start using it to store our stuff.

Not to worry though. I think I have the solution to our dilemma. What I think we need is a good pandemic. If we can just get a good breakout of bubonic plague or smallpox, we can kill off a good percentage of the population. Then we'll be able to get rid of their stuff. I think maybe I'll go out and stockpile a bunch of antibiotics and put 'em in my public storage unit. That way, when the breakout occurs, I can use my stockpile to survive. All those hoarders without my forethought, will die. I'll have more room for all my stuff. But I'm truly glad that I'm only renting that storage locker; this way, when I eventually do die, they can easily clean it out, no probate, just a quick sale of items and just move on to the next tenant.

What's In A Name?

The Social Security Administration recently came out with their annual list of most popular names. I have to say, I think there's still hope out there for our future. The names that topped the 2016 list were Noah, Liam, William, Mason, and James for boys, and Emma, Olivia, Ava, Sophia, and Isabella for girls. While there's certainly nothing wrong with the John's and Jane's of the world, there is something to be said for names that are not too common yet not too weird. I'm proud of the parents of these recent babies.

I've always been pretty happy with my name, Leslie. Although I've had some confusion in my life over the fact that it is both a male and a female name, it has otherwise served me well. When it came time for me to name my first child I tried to take a lot of things into account. How would her name sound with our last name? What would her initials be? How would it be spelled? At first, we wanted to name her Amanda. Always wanting to assume what nickname she might be called, we made the leap that she would probably have gone by Mandy. I had visions of the first day of school. With the last name Handler, I thought the kids might make fun of her and call her Mandy Handy. The name Amanda flew out the door in a jiffy.

I don't quite understand why expecting parents don't take their last name into consideration when they are naming their children. There's a news co-anchor by the name of Krystal Ball. At first, I thought that perhaps this was an unfortunate name she took through marriage, but a Google search corrected my error. I knew a girl in high school by the name of Rosey Rose and once read about men named Rich White and Ben Dover. Really? When their parents named them Richard and Benjamin, did they not take into account that they'd be called Rich and Ben? If so, did they not know what their own last names were? There was even a Texas governor by the name of Hogg who named his own daughter Ima. I swear...you can Google it. Ask North West about her name in a few years.

Then you have to take into account what the poor kids initials are going to be. David Matthew Vaneli has to live with "DMV" for the rest of his life. Lisa Olivia Lockhart will be "LOL," and Pamela Maria Susskind will forever have "PMS." People, you have nine months to make a decision. Think carefully!

I can tell you of three places to avoid when trying to name a child: the hospital, the cemetery, and any type of disaster. When I was a kid, I often waited in hospital waiting rooms while my father, a doctor, made his rounds. I can clearly recall the pages that went out over the intercom: "paging Dr. Doctor, Dr. Doctor, please call extension 519." I'm not lying! There was a dermatologist in town by the name of Dr. Cheek, some kind of specialist named Dr. Pain, and I've recently heard about a chiropractor by the name of Will Tickle. Of course you never know what profession your child may go into, but seriously, even if he wasn't a chiropractor, Will Tickle???

The cemetery is the place you should stay away from when attempting to come up with names. The tombstones have ancient names that just won't do today. My own Grandparents were Matilda and Milton. Can you imagine a little toddler running around with their little toddler body and the face of old man Milton? How about Bertha or Murray? Poor little old baby.

Disasters both natural and otherwise should also be avoided. Are you honestly planning on naming your child Floyd, Katrina, Sandy, or Harvey? What's next? 9/11 Smith and Newtown Johnson?

If you have a word for a name such as Handler, Picker, or Still please don't give your kid a word for a first name too. I wouldn't name a son Manny. He'd have to go through life as a Man Handler. So please, if your last name is Picker, don't name your daughter Daisy or Nose, and if your last name is Still, don't name your son Stan.

Maybe that's why some famous people don't even have last names. Maybe Cher's last name is Raid, maybe Bono's last name is Fide, and maybe Prince's last name was Charming. Who knows? They're too embarrassed to tell us.

Nicknames are fine as long as formal one's are also in place. I really don't care to do business with a forty-year-old man named Skippy.

Even I fell victim to this one: spelling. My youngest is Nicki. Nicole is just fine to her, but she hates the "c" in her nickname. But please call her up for me and tell her it's not as bad as Kristoffer, Danyal, Aleeysha, or Izobelle.

Your child is not a month of the year: April, May, or June. Nor is she plant life: Petunia, Violet, or Ivy. And must we have feelings for names such as Hope, Faith, and Serenity? If so, go for the gold. Name your kid Doubt, Despair, or Storm. You could even spell them Douwt, Deespare, or Storem. Wouldn't that be special? I 'll try not to judge where the parents were when they named their daughter Bubbles, Trixie, or DeeLite.

For those of you in the throes of baby naming, I wish you a happy, healthy baby. Please honor him or her by thinking through the name you choose.

Standing in Line

We all have to wait our turn in line on a regular basis. We wait to pay for our morning coffee in the cafeteria. We wait to pump our gas. We wait in line at the grocery store. We wait in line at the deli counter, and we always, always wait in line to get into the ladies' room.

I had an epiphany recently while waiting in a line. My epiphany was that I came to the conclusion that lines are too random in this country. This makes them unfair, and even though our parents told us since we were little kids that life isn't fair, we still want it to be.

Isn't the idea of a line supposed to inherently be fair by allowing each person to take his or her turn in an orderly and reasonably fair fashion? Perhaps not because when I recently found myself third in line at a cafeteria after progressing from tenth in line, the management decided to open up a new checkout lane. So all the people behind me got to check out before me. Not being a saint myself, I admit this frustrated me. But my parents did tell me that life isn't fair.

When I recently went to pump gas, I found that all the pumps were full, so I tried to wait at the edge of the parking area in order to pull in to the first available pump. I was not successful. Two cars pulled in after me and pulled right up behind other cars to wait for them to complete their transactions. When I got the hint, I chose a lane and pulled up behind a person pumping as well. But as two more drivers pulled up behind two more pumping customers, I found that I ended up being the last to obtain my turn to pump my gas. I guess you can call it the luck of the draw, or bad line karma. So I tried to shake it off. After all, we're not supposed to sweat the small stuff, and my parents always told me that life isn't fair.

Then I was on to the grocery store. Here too, I have a line dilemma. I can get into the fifteen items or less line, behind the person with thirty items or more, I can go into the self-checkout area, and listen to the register tell me over and over to wait for someone to assist me (why do they call these things "self-checkout" again?), or I can make an attempt at standing in the shortest line behind the person with the least number of items in their cart. I always choose wrong. I've even stood in line and turned to the person behind me on a number of occasions to suggest to them that they stand in another line because the line I always choose is the "whine line." You know, it's the one in which the person in front of you invariably has to whine about the price of produce, the store coupon policy, or the fact that they forgot their milk and need to make everyone else wait while they go to get it. But I admit it, my parents did tell me that life wasn't fair.

Hey what about that guy at the deli counter who sees three other people waiting their turn when he takes a number? He proudly waves it at the deli clerk and says his number is up next, ahead of the folks he clearly saw were already waiting. Fair? My parents told me life wasn't fair.

Now I realize that this issue I have with lines and the lack of fairness while standing in them is a first world problem and not one to be taken with too much seriousness, but I do feel I have cause for concern. If lines were more fair, perhaps there would be just a little more patience between our fellow shoppers, and a little more kindness to go around...even if life isn't fair.

Scrub Daddy

More than anything, I hope I'm just like a Scrub Daddy. You know, one of those sponge things shaped like a smiley face that scrubs things with a hard outer core when you put it in cold water and a soft cushy inner core when you put it in hot water. Yep, I want to be just like one of them. I've seen them in orange, green, and yellow. I don't really care which color. Maybe I'll change colors like wearing a different outfit every day. You know: wash one, wear one, have one in reserve.

I bought my very first package of them from Bed Bath and Beyond several months ago, and I've never looked back. They help me clean just about everything around the house. "That's cool," you may say, "but why do you want to be like one?"

I want to be like one because of my friend Sheila, with whom I am no longer friends, and because of my ex-friend Janet. Sheila was one of those people I thought I could relate to. When I was down about something, she would commiserate with me. Misery loves company, so she was my go to person when I was miserable. Being the good friend that I was, I too, was her go to under the same circumstances. The problem was that Sheila was always under those circumstances. Everything in her life was terrible. If she stubbed her toe in the morning, it was a bad thing, but if she also clogged the toilet in the same day, the day was a complete disaster and the week wasn't looking so hot either. God help the world if she ever got more than a cold or one of her kids ended up being cut from the team. I truly hope that no true tragedy ever befalls Sheila because she would not be able to handle it. She would completely fall apart. I had to stop seeing her because she was poison to me. She was the most negative person I knew, and she could bring me right down with her. One reason I want to be like a Scrub Daddy is because of her.

The other reason is because of my ex-friend Janet. Janet had a tough life. She was on her own by the time she was seventeen. She raised her younger siblings herself, put herself through college and grad school, and got herself a great job. I really admired what she accomplished in life. But when I would try to go out to lunch with her, she would almost always send her food back. It wasn't just that she sent it back. She yelled at the waiter while doing it. She would cut in line everywhere we went, and had something bad to say about everyone. I had to stop seeing her because she was poison to me too. She was the most obnoxious person I knew, and she would embarrass me whenever I went out with her. She had accomplished so much in life, including a very hard impenetrable exterior. The second reason I want to be like a Scrub Daddy is because of her.

I don't want to be like Sheila, I don't want to fall apart over every little thing. I don't even want to fall apart over the big things. I want to be strong, I want to be able to deal with life as it comes. But unlike Janet, I don't want to be so strong that I've hardened to life and never let the good in. Nope, I want to be like Scrub Daddy: hard when the water's cold, soft when the water's warm, strong enough to tackle most anything, and always smiling!

Woman vs. Food

I've seen the show "Man vs. Food" on TV. Don't judge. I only watched it because my husband has control of the TV flipper at all times. It's a requirement. When we took our vows, it was part of the deal. I had to love, honor, cherish, and relinquish all rights to the TV flipper. But that's beside the point.

The point is that if they can make a show called "Man vs. Food," then I think they should be able to make a show called "Woman vs. Food." But the premise would be completely different. I don't want to see a woman eating anyone into oblivion. What I do want to see is a show that regularly interviews the man on the street about women and the food they smell like. Now I like my spritz of perfume as much as the next lady, but I want to smell like flowers, not food. I'm not looking to be eaten.

Why is it that every time I want to wash my hands in a public lady's room, which of course is every time, I am forced to use soap that smells like strawberries, or cinnamon, lemons, or cupcakes? They say you have to sing the birthday song two times in a row to know that you've washed your hands for long enough. I've taken to singing four times in a row without soap, I figure if you're good at math, that makes us even. If you're bad at math, it doesn't matter, because singing twice while using cupcake-scented soap still doesn't equate to my getting to actually eat a cupcake. I rarely use the soap in public. I just don't want to smell like food.

So getting back to the show, it would stop men on the street to interview them in a blind smell test. First, they'd have to smell the woman who lathered up with food soap. Then they'd have to smell the woman who washed with plain water, but spritzed a little floral perfume when she dressed that day. Then people call into the show. Well, I do want the show to be successful, and reality TV is all the rage today. So people call into the show and place their bets on whether the male tester prefers the scent of the woman (no this is not a remake of the movie *Scent of a Woman)* with the food smelling soap, or if he prefers the scent of the woman with the little floral perfume spritz.

What do you want to bet, that nine times out of ten, the survey says men prefer the food smell? And they say the way to get to a man's heart is through his stomach. Ha!

Murphy's

Hello. Please allow me to introduce myself to you. My name is Murphy's. Murphy's Law. Yep, that's me. You can blame it on me. It's ok. I don't mind. Really. If it's bad, and it happened. It's my fault. It's the law.

Go ahead. Blame me.

You can blame me for the term "going postal". In the eighties, I lived in a town called Edmond, Oklahoma. There was one main post office in Edmond. It was my post office. At that post office, a former employee walked in and murdered fourteen postal workers. Many more were injured. It was the first time the term "going postal" was ever used. Go ahead, Google it. It happened because I lived there in the eighties. I know it did.

Go ahead. Blame me.

You can blame me for 9/11 too. Yes. You absolutely can. You see, the August before 9/11 we bought a brand new high definition TV. But there was very little high definition programming available at the time. We were about to celebrate our eighteenth wedding anniversary, so I decided as a special present for my husband, I was going to have an antennae installed on the roof of our house that could pick up the HD channels from the top of the World Trade Towers fifteen miles away. Therefore, two weeks later, 9/11 happened. It happened because I bought something that required the towers to be there. I know it did.

Go ahead. Blame me.

You can blame me for the terrible snowy winter we had in 2013 too. You see, two and a half years before, I finally purchased a snow blower. So of course, for two winters in a row, we barely got any snow. So I sold the snow blower. Therefore, the first winter we had post sale, the 2nd snowiest winter on record occurred. It happened because I sold the snow blower. I know it did.

Go ahead. Blame me.

You'd think I'd get used to it by now, but I'm not. You see, I never carry a purse. I also don't know one designer from another. This week, we're having a designer Bag Bingo night to raise money for charity. What do you want to bet, I win the most expensive designer bag of the evening?

Go ahead. Blame me now.

P.S. We did have that fund-raiser a few days after I wrote this piece. I won the bag. I gave it to my mom.

Words

Words have always amazed me. I'm fascinated each year when I hear the list of new words that have actually entered the dictionary as acceptable. The recently added words of "twerk" and "selfie" make sense to me. They've been in our lexicon for only a short time and got voted in by the mysterious panel of dictionary judges.

But I have a few bones to pick with the judging panel when I question the following four words added to the dictionary recently: do-over, wackadoodle, demo, and E ticket.

Allow me to elaborate one at a time.

Do-over: Really? We've had do-overs for decades. I can confirm with my parents that do-overs were being done over in golf, baseball, stick ball, and extra credit school reports since before the 1950's. This is seriously only just now, an accepted word?

Wackadoodle: It took the dictionary folk until 2014 to add this to the list? Maybe they should add themselves to the definition. Last year's spell check doesn't like this one either.

Demo: Ok, I'll give them a little slack on this one. I feel sure the real word was demonstration, but we were making demos before mixed tapes came and went.

E ticket: Again, I'll give them a little slack here, but only for the definition. Today's definition refers to a ticket that may be purchased online. However, in the mid-twentieth century, an E ticket was the prized ticket to be had to go on the best Disney rides in the park. If you didn't know that, ask anyone over the age of....well, a person older than you.

Then there are a few words that have been in the dictionary for a while that shocked me. Two that come to mind are "c'mon" and "ya'll." I couldn't believe my eyes when I saw that c'mon was a legitimate contraction listed in the dictionary. But most shocking of all, was when I laid eyes on the word "ya'll". In 1983, when I married my Yankee husband, we had an argument about the legitimacy of the word "ya'll". At the time, I used it all the time. We looked it up in my college dictionary.

My husband won the argument. I can't wait to tell him the good news when he gets home tonight!

After educating myself on the latest and greatest acceptable words to use in the English language, I am now pondering why three of my favorites, have yet to make it to the list: "yabut," "sup," and "dija."

Yabut (pronounced like the first two syllables of Fred Flintstone's "yabadabadoo" with a "t" on the end) is used daily by people of all walks of life. It's a new form of language. It's not actually a contraction so perhaps it should be called a combo action defining a combination of two words: "yes" and "but."

Sup is of course short for "what's up", but the only definition found in the dictionary is the past tense of the word sip.

Dija is another combo action word. It means "did you," and is frequently used when one is nudging the arm of the person they are speaking to. It is often used in the form of a question. "Dija see that? Well dija?"

All and all, I personally believe they need me on the judging panel for next year.

Call The Grammar Police. Paleeze!

Sup w u? Ur sis called. C u 2nite.

This was a recent text I sent. I may be a boomer, but I can still text with the best of 'em...as long as I'm still allowed to write when it's necessary. I do worry; however, that proper grammar is becoming a completely lost art.

I recently read an article written on the topic of the abandonment of the essay to the SAT college entrance exams. It got me thinking about the state of the written word today. I love writing. It's a passion of mine. But I do understand that for many, it's a painful source of frustration. As I write this, I keep thinking about my own grammatical issues. I have a problem with tenses. I know there's a past, present, and future tense, but did you know that there are others? There's the simple present, the present perfect, the present continuous, and even the present perfect continuous. That's just for starters. I have a terrible time with these. Thank God I have an awesome editor who makes me look good, because it can get intense (pun totally intended). But as bad as I am at grammar (and puns), I now realize that there are others who are much worse than I.

If your grammar is bad theirs always someone worse and if your good at it thats because this sentence drives you crazy.

There are six errors in that sentence. As I said, I can be just as guilty as the next guy when it comes to poor grammar, but I've been amazed at the common errors I've seen out in public lately. If you ask me, some of them show just a little too much cleavage.

The following is a sign I recently saw posted online:

Seat Belts must be worn

Doors must be shut

Its the Law

And how about this one:

Perfection has It's Price

How would you like to order this off the breakfast menu?

Includes eggs, toast and orange juice.

I don't know about you, but I like my toast dry and not mixed in with my OJ. For those of you who don't get it, this is where the "oxford" comma comes into play. Without the comma, you could read this as one who wants toast in their juice; with the comma, it's clear that they are desired separately. Most newspapers no longer use the oxford comma, also known as the serial comma, but I still cling to it for the following reason.

If I were to say "My parents, Beyoncé and Jay-Z, love going to the movies," you might think that my parents are Beyoncé and Jay-Z. But if I use the comma and write "My parents, Beyoncé, and Jay-Z love going to the movies, then you'd understand that I was speaking about my parents and two other people. Sorry for the punctuation lesson ya'll, but this is a big deal to me.

I wonder if the writers of the following sentences understood the meaning of what was actually written.

Remember in prayer the many who are sick of our community.

For those of you who have children and don't know it, we have a nursery downstairs.

Please place your donation in the envelope along with the deceased person you want remembered.

The last three really make me laugh, but at the same time, they make me sad. In an era in which the teaching of typing has replaced the teaching of cursive, has texting displaced proper grammar? What am I to think when I go to buy fish and they tell me that it's "fresh frozen"? Well is it fresh, or is it frozen? And what about the infomercial touting their product as "genuine faux"? Is it genuine or not?

Test your skills on a few of my pet peeves:

Is it affect or effect?

Should you use like or such as?

All of a sudden or all of the sudden?

Who or Whom?

The good news, is that my spell check tried to correct most of the errors in the bloopers I used in this piece. The bad news, is that it only caught most of them.

This essay was first published in *Boomercafe*. I enjoyed some of the post publication comments. I hope you do too.

One Reader said:

My favorite would be "New and Improved!" OK, which is it? Is it new, or is it last month's   model that someone has "improved"?

My Response:

Ah yes. "New and improved" is a winner. I'll add it to one of my other favorites: stop light. Is it a stop sign or a traffic light? Where's the "go light?"

Isn't this fun?

Another Reader Posted:

Hi Leslie, I appreciate your passion for good writing. I love to write, too. But, it is an   ongoing learning process. Also, I fight with my text "auto correct" on my cell phone and   the word choices the program selects.

My Response:

I feel your pain. That's why I'm able to reply to you here. I agree. I'll put on my boxing gloves for e-mails, but I've accepted my collection of tickets from the grammar police regarding texts. "Sup, u, luv, btw, etc r all grammatically correct in the new and improved genuine faux Handler Texting pocket guide to proper grammar and spelling.

Then I added:

C that, the "p" and the "g" should be capitalized. Can u feel my shame?

And Finally from a Reader:

I used to teach grammar and I pride myself on having raised a son who uses "who" or   "whom" correctly.

My Reply:

Thank you from the bottom of my heart. Perhaps there is still hope for our future generations.

Presidential Candidacy

I could never run for president: too many skeletons in the closet. I'm a thieving, crime breaking, citizen who would never survive being vetted. I've sampled the grapes before paying for them. I am a thief. I've smoked and even inhaled. You can arrest me for drug possession. I've bought and killed an untold number of plants in my lifetime. I am a mass murderer. I told my kids they couldn't eat dessert unless they first ate their vegetables. I am an extortionist.

Upon even further pondering, I may not even be a US citizen as it is a fact that my father spoke Hungarian before he spoke English. We've had a Catholic president, a black president, and almost had our first female president, but I don't think the country is ready for its first thieving, drug possessed, mass murdering, extortionist.

Then again, unlike our current congress, I do know how to compromise since I can verify that I've lived with a person of the opposite sex for over thirty years. Actually, this might make me an American hero.

Perhaps I'll run in 2020 after all.

<u>Chapter Seven: Body Image</u>

I didn't eat 'em. Really!

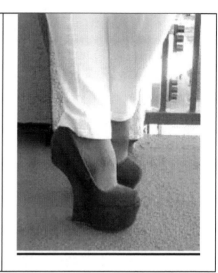

Yes, they were selling these in stores. Women actually bought them!

Life happened to me. I started gaining weight. It was only a little at first. Then it was a lot. One morning I woke up and I was over one hundred pounds overweight. Now this would be bad enough for a normal person, but for me, at only five foot two inches, one hundred plus pounds was overwhelming. I was recovering from cancer surgery number x?x? (there have been so many, I lost count long ago), and I found myself on anti-depressants, pain meds, blood pressure meds, and a sleep apnea machine. By now, I was well over forty and not the sexiest woman alive. Poor Marty rolled over at night to see a whale lying next to him with an elephant trunk coming out of a breathing apparatus. He never complained. I wish I could tell you what my "aha" moment was, but I can't. What I can tell you is that I had been overweight for almost twenty years, and seeing that huge number on the scale day after day wasn't helping. Over the years, I had tried every diet out there. I also had tried every excuse out there as to why I couldn't lose the weight. Then one day, I just sat down and had a chat with myself. I tried to figure it out. Although I have yet to quite

94

make it to my goal weight, I am very close. I lost eighty pounds over two and a half years. I've kept it off for five years.

Boob One and Boob Two

After two wallet thefts within a six-month time frame, I decided to give up carrying a purse. So where was I to carry my wallet and my cell phone? Pockets? I don't know about you, but I don't always have an outfit with pockets. So I spent some time contemplating what to do. My epiphany came when I realized that there is one item that I wear every day without fail. I never ever leave home without it. So unless I want my boobs to hang down as far as my falling gynecological parts do, I ain't leavin' the house without a bra.

You're welcome.

Problem solved. You will now find me on any given day, with my cell phone in one bra cup, and my wallet in the other. Thus, please let me know what you think of my following solution while I thank Dr. Seuss for the inspiration.

Did you ever hear of boob one and boob two?

They sit on my chest and they look out at you.

On each side of one, is an arm and a hand.

Two is the same, they're a pair, they are grand.

Most days on the arm of boob one could be found,

a purse hanging down, it was red. It was round.

A stranger broke in and with fingers so light,

she took out my wallet, no struggle, no fight.

Nowadays it's easier for boob one and boob two,

they don't have to put up with that purse that was new.

Boob one has the credit. Boob two has the phone.

I can give you a call. I can make you a loan.

I can now walk with pride with boob one and boob two,

for I don't have to carry a purse now. Do you?

What Price, Vanity?

I recently decided that I was due for an eyebrow plucking. I haven't quite decided why this is important for women to do and not for men. Was it vanity lurking or simply good hygiene?

Whatever the case, I decided that I was overdue. In my youth, I would grab a tweezer, lean over the bathroom sink, peer into the mirror, and pluck out a few stray hairs. Mission accomplished.

When I turned forty, I discovered that I needed glasses to see in order to get the job done. So I plunked down the cash for a new pair and was then able to set forth on my monthly mission to rid myself of the offending hairs.

Last month, even with my glasses, I just couldn't see to accomplish the task at hand, so I grabbed the car keys and headed for the nearest salon to pay for both the plucking and the tip (don't forget the cost of gas to get there).

This month, I tried to be frugal. I went out and bought a hand mirror that has a ten-time magnification. I was so proud of myself as I plucked away to rid myself of those pesky strays. But then I noticed two things I hadn't noticed before:

1) I was plucking lots of gray hairs. They were in the right places, but they were gray, so of course, they had to be plucked.

and

2) I had lots of crepey, droopy, wrinkly, skin that encircled my eyes.

After several minutes of serious plucking, I found that I'd plucked so many grays that I now had to go out and buy an eyebrow pencil to draw back in the now missing hairs: more gas, more beauty supplies.

But that's not all. Now I also need an eye lift to get rid of the crepey, droopy, wrinkles I hadn't known were there before. My wallet is empty. Ladies, heed my advice. If you ever want to have enough money to retire on, for heaven sake, don't pluck your eyebrows!

How's That Been Workin' for Ya?

Please allow me to preface my words by first stating that I am not a doctor. I am not a psychologist, a life coach, or a personal trainer. What I am, is a person who has figured it out. I've lost over eighty pounds. I still have about twenty-five to my goal, but I have zero doubt that I will eventually get there. I also know that I will keep it off forever.

I spent twenty years being obese. I've heard it all because I've said it all. I've said it out loud to others. Worse, I've said it to myself. "I just can't lose weight. Diets don't work for me." Well half that statement is right. The other, is absurd. But I believed it. I believed I couldn't lose weight. I believed I was destined to remain fat forever. I believed the first sentence because the second sentence was true. Here's the new revelation: diets don't work for anyone.

Well let me correct myself just a bit. If you have ten pounds or less to lose and you want to get a little weight off for your big upcoming event, then a diet just might do the trick. For all the rest of us, it's time to celebrate Burnivus: the festival celebrating the burning of all diet books ever published.

I've read diet books on what foods to eat. I've read books on what portions to eat. I've read books about what exercises to do. I've even read books written by skinny people telling me how to think about food. I say burn them all. None of them tell you the real thing you need to know if you truly want to lose weight, lose it in a healthy way, and lose it forever.

So here it is. Are you ready? Here's what people pay big bucks to know. You have to figure out what's going on between your ears. You've got to use your brain. We're all so quick to run to the nearest diet center, buy the newest book, and follow the newest diet craze. We're all too willing to plunk down our hard earned dollars for someone to weigh us, package food for us, prescribe a pill for us, and teach us the latest exercise craze. We have the firm belief in our heads that if we just pay the right people the right amount of money, they'll be able to make it happen. It will be worth all that money if they can just make it work for us.

I beg you, listen to what's going on between your ears. You have a brain. I know you do. It's in there somewhere. It's above your hands that are holding the latest diet book, and it's above your mouth full of fudgy brownies. The only thing on top of it is your hair, if you still have any.

Stop the madness I say. Stop paying someone else to think for you. Please, use your noggin. Allow me to explain what I mean. First I need you to understand how good we are in using our minds to make excuses for ourselves. How many times have you said to yourself that you have a slow metabolism? How many times have you said that you have a Thyroid problem? How many times have you told yourself that you were just born with bad genes? Have you told yourself you can't lose weight because of the medication you're on? Granted, it's possible that you do have one or even all of these problems. So when's the last time you marched yourself into the doctor's office to have it all checked out? My guess is that the answer to that question is never. If you feel you truly have a medical reason why you are overweight, then why wouldn't you get it checked out? Perhaps because not knowing is working for you. Perhaps it's giving you the perfect excuse to do nothing and remain overweight.

Another of the excuses I've heard are people who tell me they're good all week long and only indulge a little on the weekends. They can't understand why they aren't losing weight. Has that plan of attack been working for you? And finally, I've heard the excuse of people telling me that they know what works for them if they really want to lose weight. They know they just have to buckle down and limit those calories and the weight will come flying off. They know how to do it better than any of the experts. They know that if they just go by the philosophy of calories in/calories out, they will lose weight. Now although this last one is technically true, how many people do you know who have cut their calories down to minuscule numbers, lost weight over an extended period of time, and kept it off?

Use your heads people, not your wallets. Go to the doctor, rid yourself of excuses. Using Your Brain 101 is to stop making excuses for yourself. Now on to Using Your Brain 102. If you do what you've always done, you'll get what you've always gotten. How many diets have you been on over the years? How many did you stick with? Did you get all the weight off you desired? Have you kept it off? If you answered that you've been on more than one diet, and you answered no to all the rest of the questions, why would you do it again the same way? Why start yet another diet and deprive yourself of all your food joy only to find that after using all willpower on the planet, you have still, in the end, failed miserably? Why? Why? Why? Use that matter you have between your ears. It never worked before. Why would it work now if you haven't changed anything? Do you honestly think that if you buy this book, learn this diet, follow this exercise routine, that this time it will magically work? I can tell you that it won't. More importantly, you can tell you that it won't.

So start thinking. What do you have to do differently this time to make it work? Concentrate. If you are anything like me, and my guess is that we are extremely alike, the one thing you always do is jump in with all the motivation in the world. You plunge in feet first, not head first, motivated to finally do it this time. You're going to be perfect. You're strong. You have awesome willpower. You want this more than anything. Let's go, let's go, let's go!

Here's where you have to put on the brakes. Here's where you have to stop and think. Haven't you been this motivated before? What went wrong? What derailed you? What made that train that was going full steam ahead suddenly lurch to a complete and utter stop and right in the middle of the tracks? Wait, go back. There was a word in there. I think I heard it. Yep, I heard it: perfect. Ah, yes, that was the word. How many people do you know who are perfect? I know I'm not, are you? Just what makes our brains think that this time we're going to be perfect? News flash: there's no such thing as being perfect all the time. I'll bet you've tried to be perfect before. I'll bet you even were perfect for a little while. But perfect can't last. The sooner you get your brain to realize this, the sooner you will be on your way to permanent weight loss. Stop with the all or nothing mentality. Stop being perfect all week because look what happens on the weekend when you let your guard down. Stop cutting calories to the bone for long periods of time because eventually, you'll give in. We all know that when that happens, if it's not nailed down, we'll eat it. Just plain stop being on a diet every day of your life. This is what caused me to finally understand what they mean when they tell you to make a lifestyle change. You have to change your thinking from either being on a diet when you restrict what you eat or off a diet when you get to eat whatever you want. Find the middle ground. The sooner you find it, the faster you'll get to your ultimate healthy weight. Allow yourself small indulgences on a regular basis. Allow yourself to be satisfied. Take baby steps towards healthy living instead of jumping in all at once. It takes months to form a single good habit. Change them one at a time.

Using your brain allows you to stop making excuses, stop doing the same unsuccessful things over and over again, and stop trying to be perfect. There's one more thing you need to use your brain for if you want to succeed in permanent weight loss. Speak kindly to yourself. It's a simple idea, but how many of us actually practice it? Think of it this way, if you spoke to your best friend the way you speak to yourself, would they still be your best friend? How many times do you tell yourself that you screwed up, you're worthless, you can't succeed, or you'll never be as _____ as someone else? Teach yourself to be kind to yourself. Instead of berating yourself, try to compliment yourself. "Wow, I ate well for one whole meal, look at me go." "Gee, I ate three different vegetables today, good for me." The list can go on forever.

Using your brain is free, and I can tell you without a doubt, that it works better than the most expensive diets out there. If you haven't been using it, how's that been workin' for ya?

Skinny People and Fat People

In this world, there are skinny people and fat people. Personally, I don't believe that physical appearance has one single thing to do with whether you are a fat person or a skinny person. I think it all has to do with what's between your ears. Allow me to explain.

When I was growing up, my family went on a whirlwind tour of Europe. My older brother kept a diary of the whole trip. All these years later, we always have a good laugh when we talk about that diary. It went something like this:

Day One: Dear Diary, we arrived in Paris today. We saw the Eiffel Tower. For breakfast I had Eggs Benedict with strawberries in cream. For lunch I had a chef's salad. For dinner I had escargot as an appetizer, chateaubriand for my main course, and cherries jubilee for dessert.

Day Two: Dear Diary, we spent the day in Rome today. We saw the Coliseum. I had a continental breakfast with a croissant and fresh butter. For lunch I had a tuna sandwich. For dinner I ate spaghetti with meatballs.

It was hysterical. Our family ate its way through Europe. To this day, my husband laughs when my parents come to visit because at dinner they are discussing what we will have for breakfast in the morning and in the morning, they are discussing what we should plan for dinner.

Being Jewish alone will cause anyone a bit of food trauma. All holidays are surrounded by food. As the Jewish motto goes, "we suffered, we survived, let's eat!"

What I'm trying to say here, is that my family is a family of fat people. Some of us are physically thin, and some of us are physically fat, but all of us, have food on the brain. We lost my grandmother many years ago, but I can still clearly hear her voice repeating the phrases she most frequently uttered.

1. Before a meal: "Jeet"? (definition: did you eat?)

2. After a meal: "You have ample?" (I think this one is self-explanatory.)

3. Five minutes after a meal: "Jeet"?

Now my husband, his family is full of skinny people. His family would've gone to Europe and kept diaries of all the sites they'd seen and the people they'd met. Today, my husband has, for the first time, developed a little baby pot belly. This does not, and I repeat, does not, make him a fat person. He's a skinny person. I'm the fat person. Here's why.

One day, we went to the grocery together. We were making all the necessary purchases when my husband made an impulse purchase of a package of double stuffed Oreo cookies. We went home and unloaded the groceries into the pantry. Every day for a week, those cookies called to me. At first it was just a little whisper.

"Leslie, we're here."

Then they got more insistent.

"Leslie, we're here. Come eat us."

Then they started screaming at me.

"WHY HAVEN'T YOU EATEN US?"

Finally, they took action and poured themselves a cold glass of milk and set it out on the counter.

"Leslie, we're ready for dunking now."

After an entire week of suffering to prevent myself from eating my husband's cookies, I just couldn't take it anymore. I finally told my husband to eat his stupid cookies or I was going to throw them away (for full disclosure, I don't think I used the actual word "stupid" here but more of a stronger, less ladylike word).

Do you know what his response was to me? Can you imagine what he said? He told me that he forgot we bought them. He forgot!!!!!!!

Now that's a skinny person for ya.

In my next life, when my mother goes to get me a warm chocolate chip cookie to make me feel better when I skin my knee on the playground, I know exactly what I'm going to do. I'm going to tape it to my knee. Yep, I'll put it right over the wound. I'll put it there instead of eating eat because it will be my understanding that it's to be put on my skinned knee to make it feel better. How on earth would eating it make me feel better? This will be my understanding about comfort food in my next life. Because in my next life, I'm determined to be a skinny person.

Retail Therapy? Humbug

As a child, I dumped out piles of new clothes onto my bed. I was exhausted after a day of school clothes shopping only to come home to the chore of cutting off tags and finding hangers to place the newly found garments in their proper place in my closet. It was a major annual event that other girls seemed to enjoy. I hated it.

To me, it was an unpleasant task-something that had to be survived. I'm all of five foot two. I don't technically know how high the racks are, but it always seemed to me that they were set on six foot legs. I had to reach up and raise my arms to their maximum extension in order to rifle through racks of clothes. As each hanger squeaked across the rod it was like another bullet came out of the rifle. Bang! That one whizzed by. Bang! Another one whizzed by. Those hangers banged and squeaked, and whizzed until I could finally find enough items that seemed acceptable enough to take back to the dressing room. Then my arms would feel like they were going to fall off from the weight of all the items I had chosen. Who needed to lift weights or do yoga stretching exercises? I did all the lifting and stretching needed just to get to the dressing room. Then the yanking of the clothes would commence. First I had to yank everything I wore off. Then I had to try on the assemblage one by one. Invariably I'd bring in all the same size, but one blouse was too small. I needed the bigger size. The pair of pants was too large. I needed a smaller size. And the sweater, well it just wasn't going to work at all. It was an endless day of yanking, and tugging, and rifling, and bullets. Arms up. Arms down. Step in. Step out.

Then there were the lights. There were always the lights. There were too many, and they were always too hot. They seared into me with their wicked eyes peering and burning, and shrinking what self-esteem I came with into the little that I left with. Eventually, I emerged out of the dressing room with a pile of clothes that were acceptable to both me and my mom. Mom paid the bill. I carted the bags of clothes home and began the task of the bed dumping and the tag removal as I wiped my brow with the happy thought that I had another year before I had to repeat the process.

As I became an adult, I had to shop alone. This meant I had to foot the bill myself. This was usually the last thing I wanted to spend my money on. I hated it even more. I never quite understood why women willingly flocked to the stores to put themselves through this torture and then called it retail therapy. I'd rather pay for a root canal in a dirty dentist's office with no anesthesia and no insurance.

Then I became a mom. As it turns out, a mom to two daughters. One had the genes of most young girls. "Mommy, can we go shopping today?" The other, poor thing, ended up with my genes. "Oh, mom, really the clothes I have are just fine." Either way, the girls needed clothes, and I was the one who had to take them shopping. I tried hard to have patience while shopping with them. I admit that it wasn't quite as bad buying things for them as it had always been for me. They had beautiful bodies with lovely taste, and who doesn't want to "do" for their children? But invariably, I'd find some new offending clothing item at the back of their closets a year later with the tags still on and I'd realize that I did still hate shopping.

After years of life itself, I found myself one hundred pounds overweight. Try shopping now! I had created a monster. Remember the drug commercial? The one with the egg frying in the pan. "This is your brain. This is your brain on drugs?" Well that was me when I was shopping. This was my brain. This was my brain while shopping. The phrase living nightmare regularly came to mind. I hope my husband appreciated this little idiosyncrasy in his wife. I hope he appreciated that he was a rare breed of husband who could actually brag about the fact that his wife was not a shopaholic.

Eventually, I got disgusted with my weight and decided to lose it for good. So I did two things. I began to lose weight, and I began to set an envelope aside with money in it. I would regularly stash away a little bit of cash at a time, each extra dollar being added to the last and being placed ever so carefully in the envelope. One day, I sat down with pen in hand, and labeled the envelope "skinny clothes fund."

Thus it has gone for the past few years. A little extra cash comes in. The envelope comes out. The cash goes in it. The envelope gets put away. After the first year, fifty of the one hundred pounds came off. My clothes were falling off of me. But my rule was that I wasn't allowed to touch the skinny clothes fund until the whole one hundred pounds was off. What to do. What to do. In desperation, and admittedly with a little pride at the substantial weight loss, I ventured into Macy's for a little peek around. After several hours of shopping all in the same department of the same store, I came out a winner with a few items, three sizes smaller than I'd been wearing for years. It would be enough to get me through for a while, and I didn't die in the process. I even showed off my accomplishment to my fashion conscious daughters.

Another year later, and twenty-five more pounds lighter, the new clothes were falling off of me. Arghhh! I would have to go shopping yet again. Ok, I admit it, I didn't absolutely hate last years' shopping event. But I had no desire to spend money on more clothes when I knew good and well that I still had twenty-five more pounds to go.

That's when I made my new discovery: consignment shops and thrift stores. I had never before ventured into either. In years gone by, I had donated tons of clothes to various charity's, but I had never thought to go into any such shops to actually make a purchase. What did I think about wearing someone else's left overs?

I ventured into an upscale consignment shop. I didn't have to rifle through racks and racks of clothes. It was a small shop with a small selection. The dressing room was well lit, but there were no searing heated bulbs. I ended up coming out with a half a dozen items that were all from higher end stores than I would normally buy from. Each item was in mint condition and about half the price I would have paid had they been brand new. Score! But after an eighty- pound weight loss, I still needed more. I needed everything. Although I did feel that I deserved a pay-off for all the hard work it had taken me to get here, the skinny clothes fund was still off limits. I still have twenty-five pounds to go before I can touch that. So I left the consignment shop and wandered into my local thrift store. Now this took real patience for a gal like me: more shopping, more rifling, more outstretched arms, more hot lights, more money I had to spend. But all was not lost. Gone were the six-foot-tall racks from my childhood memory. Everything was down on racks no higher than three or four feet. Gone were the hot lights: there were no lights at all, other than the overhead lights throughout the entire store. And gone were the high prices of the department store.

I approached the register with my stack of clothes that were to get me through my last twenty- five pounds. My stash included three pairs of pants, one by Gloria Vanderbilt, four blouses, one from Ann Taylor, and three sweaters, one 100% cashmere. The total for my purchase was $40. Yes, $40!

I went home to repeat the traditional bed dumping. But this time, I was happily cutting off price tags of smaller, less expensive clothes and gently finding hangars to proudly place the newly found garments in their proper place in my closet. Instead of wiping my brow in frustration, I checked the activity monitor that I now wear regularly. To my surprise and delight, my shopping workout had earned me more daily calories burned than any other day in the history of my wearing it!

I have 25 more pounds to go, but I think that maybe, just maybe, I'm going to have fun spending my skinny clothes fund. At the very least, it will be a good aerobic workout.

Is Anybody Thinking?

Ok. I admit it. I wasn't thinking when my twenty-five-year-old daughter showed me her adorable new red suede high heeled sneakers. Yes, I did say high heeled sneakers. Technically, they're high wedges, but either way, they're shoes with laces that look like sneakers but put the wearer's foot at almost a forty- five-degree angle. I wasn't thinking because I am not twenty- five, and I ordered a pair for myself. When I wore them with jeans, they looked cute, albeit uncomfortable, but when I made an attempt at wearing them with a casual dress all hell broke loose. The dress was new, and when I went to wear it for the first time, I realized that the red suede shoes were the only ones I had that matched. When I paraded into the living room to announce to my husband that I was ready to go out, he wanted to know when I was changing. This from a man who never noticed the day I dyed my lifetime of brown hair to red.

"You don't like it," I asked?

"It's fine if you're trying to look like you're a twenty- year- old pushin' fifty," he responded.

I couldn't change fast enough. The dress didn't get worn until I purchased a new, and flatter pair of shoes. What was I thinking? Really? Sneakers with heels? Now don't misunderstand me, I'm all for keeping up with new trends, keeping active, and trying to look my best, but I want to look my best for the fifty something year old woman that I am, not one who's trying to relive my youth.

My own father was a plastic surgeon. I'm all for people going in for a tuck here or a nip there for the sake of making themselves feel better, but honestly, did Joan Rivers not know that we were aware of how long she'd been around? I don't want to be fifty trying to look twenty. I don't want to be sixty trying to look thirty. And for heaven sakes if I'm fortunate enough to live to my nineties, will I really care if I don't look seventy?

Now that I'm in my fifties, I try to find a happy medium. I don't want to go to the stores that cater to the twenty somethings, but I don't want to shop at the old lady stores either. It seems that no matter what type of clothing store I'm in, I'm trying to figure out if there's a fabric shortage in this country, or if there's a conspiracy by the fashion moguls to try to sell me more articles of clothing. What should I be thinking when the fabric of every blouse I try on is so thin that it requires me to wear a camisole underneath? I can't decide if it's the camisole manufacturers who have formed the country's strongest union, if cheap labor has created a cheaply made product that's transparent, if we have transparent clothes purposefully being made to replace the transparent government that we don't have, or if there's a nationwide conspiracy to fulfill the fetish of the men's club who has formed their memberships by recruiting members who seek middle-aged women who strut in public in see-through clothing that reveals every inch of flab she thinks she's covering up!

And please tell me who invented the "who cares if your bra strap shows or what color it is" fashion trend. I can't tell you how many blouses I've tried on in which I have yet to find any Victoria Secret bra with any type of strap adjustment that will work for it without the straps showing unless I want to permanently walk around in a strapless bra. What were they thinking when they invented strapless bras anyway? If your boobs are young and perky, you don't need one, and if they're old and droopy, let's face it, there ain't no strapless out there that's gonna lift and separate the old girls well enough for public consumption.

And don't go thinking this craziness is reserved just for women. Have you seen the half thong for men? For your own health and safety, I highly recommend you Google it. I wouldn't want you to be caught unprepared in mixed company on your first viewing of this little, and I do mean little, fashion trend. I don't know about you, but after the bris, and he if he ain't my partner, if I want to see any other man's junk, I'll call 1-800-Got-Junk for an estimate.

I don't begrudge anyone trying to look their best, but for me, I want to look my best for the middle aged/senior woman that I am. So I do admit that I was in error in trying the high heeled sneaks with the dress, but the thirty something woman I saw at the mall recently has me beat. She was donning a pair of high heels without the high heel! I'm not kidding. My jaw dropped, and my eyes bugged out, and I couldn't keep myself from staring. When I got home, I Googled new trends in shoes and found "no heel high heels" also called "anti-gravity wedges." Are you kidding me? Have you seen these things? Not only are they selling pairs of shoes in which you are literally to be walking on your toes, but women are actually buying them. What are they thinking? I don't care what decade of life you're in, the sight of these things makes me nuts.

Whatever new trends come down the pike, I'll be ready...to judge for myself, and my age, whether the trend is right for me or not, because next time I buy one single pair of shoes that aren't comfortable, I'll be going crazy. You wanna come for the ride?

Body Parts

Why do we always have such an issue with calling a spade a spade? If it's in the deck of cards, and it's not a club, a diamond, or a heart, it's a spade. See, was that so difficult? So why on earth do we have to use so many euphemisms for everything else? Why can't a person just die? Not that I want anyone to die, but when they do, can't they just be dead? Why do we always have to say they've passed away, or they've gone to a better place? We are confusing the children of America by doing this. The three year olds have started to tell us that they don't want to go to school today. They want to go to a better place.

When other women start talking about "down there," I start getting confused, and I'm not even three years old! Some call it your privates. Others tell me they are referring to the carpet as opposed to the drapes. Even Oprah used to tell us it's a "va jay jay." Honestly, I don't want anyone saluting my privates, getting out the Hoover for my carpet, or comparing any part of my anatomy to the children's airplane cartoon character from the Jay Jay the Jet Plane cartoon series.

Then of course we move on to the opposite end of the female body. You know, the boobs, the girls, the tee tas. We spend a fortune on these things. We buy bras to push them up, bras to minimize, and bras to lift and separate. But God forbid we say the word that actually goes into these expensive contraptions. Why is it that we can't just call them what they are? It's getting ridiculous. Do you know that in most school library's today, they have blocks on the internet so that kids can't even look up a recipe for chicken breasts? Oh my God, I said it: breasts.

Years ago, my dad had a secretary who told him of the time her three-year-old granddaughter came to spend the night. The only other woman the child had ever seen naked was her mother. When the grandma went to take a bath and removed all her clothing, the little girl asked her a simple question. She pointed to the upper half of her grandmother's body and said "grandma, are your breasts dead?"

Let the three year olds of America unite! Let free speech reign. Let's put death, vaginas and breasts back into the English language.

Please Remove My Granny Panties

I'm ashamed to say it. I can't believe it myself. But the following words actually came out of my mouth the other night just before I went to bed. "Dear, if I die during the night, would you please kindly remove my socks and my granny panties before they come take me away?" To his credit, my husband affirmed my request without further comment.

Also to my husband's credit, he is the least vain person I have ever met. He's neat and well groomed, but he could care less about gray hairs and wrinkles. I, on the other hand, am afflicted with the vanity gene. I fuss with my hair and make-up, match my jewelry to my outfit, and like to wear matching bras and panties. I've tried over the years not to "let myself go."

Even when I get in bed at night, I don't want to feel like an old biddy by wearing sweats and a t-shirt. My birthday suit is just fine with me if I'm home, and a nightgown is acceptable if I'm in the company of others.

But alas, there are certain times of the month and the year, when my birthday suit just won't do, and who wants to wear their pretty lace panties to bed when there's a good probability you'll wake up with a stain on them. So granny panties it is.

Then there are those nights when even the electric blanket won't warm up my feet. Thus, on go the thick warm socks.

So you can understand my dismay when I found myself going to bed with both the other night: socks and granny panties. How embarrassing it would be to have lived a lifetime of bedtimes in the raw, or at the very least in a pretty nightgown, only to find my last night on earth with socks and granny panties.

Thank God for husbands who understand these things.

A Trip to Crazy

It seems that, as I get older, I get more and more of a hitch in my giddy up. It started with a little sore ankle that never got better. Then a little plantar fasciitis was added to the mix. A sore hip became a herniated disc, followed by surgery with a splash of osteoarthritis added in. I guess these things just can't be avoided. I know I'm not alone whenever I go to get up from a lengthy seated position with friends. As each of us rises, a combined groaning sigh softly comes out of each of us as we rise and stretch out our aching body parts. It's all to be expected as we age, and as my mother-in-law used to always say "it beats the alternative."

But my cause for concern lately isn't the physical, but the mental hitches. I've always known that with the birth of each child, I lost brain cells. There was the time when I packed the new baby's bag for an outing. I made sure I had extra diapers, wipes, formula, toys, and even a change of clothes...for both of us. I got in the elevator of our high rise apartment, pushed the down button, and watched the door close as I hung that heavy diaper bag over my shoulder and realized I had everything I needed...except the baby! She was safely locked in the apartment... all by herself. That's when it all started. Then there were the times I drove off with my purse on the hood of the car, couldn't find the car keys hanging in their regular spot by the back door, couldn't find my glasses on top of my head, and couldn't remember why I walked into a room. But as I've aged, I've gotten worse.

There was the time I drove cross country with the two kids, two birds, three dogs, and a myriad of hamsters when I stopped at the half-way point for a fill-up and tried to drive off without removing the gas pump from the car. We drove the rest of the trip with trash bags taped to the rear window of the car.

There was the time I almost burned the house down not once, but twice when I built a nice fire in the fireplace leaving the flu closed.

Last month I thought my dentist was crazy. He told me that we would need to take the impression for my new mouth guard. "What mouth guard," I asked? "The one we talked about last time you were in. I have it here in my notes," he said. I insisted that we had never discussed it, but we went ahead and took the impression and ordered the guard. That night,

I told my husband that the dentist was nuts because he tried to tell me that he had discussed ordering a mouth guard with me when I knew we had never discussed it before. My husband then informed me that I told him all about a discussion I'd had with the dentist about a mouth guard the month before. Apparently it was I who was going crazy.

Then last week, I insisted that the auto repair shop got my passenger side seat all wet. I insisted that they must have spilled something all over the seat. I told them that they were responsible for the warning light that went on on my dash telling me that there was a short circuit in the passenger air bag that was caused by the seat getting wet. I insisted that they would need to both repair the problem and pay for my seat to be steamed cleaned. I woke up in the middle of the night realizing that I had placed a bottle of Gatorade inside the back pack I had on the passenger seat earlier that day. I jumped out of bed, went to where I store my back pack, felt the bottom of it was soaking wet, reached in, and pulled out a now empty bottle of Gatorade. I made my husband call the shop the next day to explain and apologize for me.

What a trip life takes us on. First my body starts to go. Then my mind completely loses its entire bag of marbles. I'm taking another trip soon. I'm going crazy. Anybody want to come for the ride?

Just One More Thing About Skinny People and Fat People

I've already told you about my weight loss and some of the things I learned along the way. Even though I've kept that weight off, I've told you that I'm still always going to be a fat person on the inside. I could be underweight (fat chance), and I'd still be a fat person. Like I've said, there are skinny people who are fat people waiting to get out. That's me.

No matter how thin I may get, I will always be out of control when it comes to chocolate. The sight of chocolate, for me, is like a starter gun going off: ready, set, eat! I've established tons of great new habits now that I'm almost at my goal weight. I keep fresh produce in the house at all times. I never let myself get hungry, and I plan ahead when eating out. I've found lots of great recipes that are healthy and fit in with my new lifestyle. Some of these recipes are dessert recipes and call for chocolate chips as one of the ingredients. My past experience with chocolate chips is a rocky road (pun completely intended). With all good intentions, I buy the ingredients for this oh-so-healthy dessert. I mix up those ingredients including the quarter of a cup of chocolate chips, and I bake the dessert. The dessert contains four servings. I eat all four. Since I've yet to find a store that sells bags of only a quarter cup of chocolate chips, I then look forward to returning to my pantry to finish off the rest of the bag. My fat person is trying to get back out. NOOOO! My solution: avoid all recipes that require chocolate chips as an ingredient.

One of the great things I learned while losing all the weight was that everything is ok in moderation. Moderation is the key. In keeping with my love of chocolate, this means that chocolate cannot forever be off limits to me. Notice that in the previous paragraph I did not say that I avoid eating chocolate or chocolate chips. I simply said that I avoid bringing an entire bag of them into my house. Another food I adore is chocolate chip cookies. Again with the chocolate chips. The good news is that I can easily purchase readymade chocolate chip cookie dough. The bad news is that my skinny body starts eating the raw dough in the car on the way home. By the time the dough actually hits the preheated oven, only half of it is left to bake.

In well less than twenty-four hours, the cooked ones have vanished. My fat person is trying to get back out. NOOOO! My solution: buy the twelve pack of cookie dough instead of the log since I'm an idiot and have no self-control. While we're on the topic of cookies, my skinny husband sees the cookies in the kitchen. Knowing that I am out of control when it comes to anything chocolate chip, he tells me to throw the remaining cookies out. He helps me by tossing them into the garbage can. But my fat person always tries to get back out. NOOOO!

My solution: Dig into the garbage can and eat the cookies. This way, they'll be all gone and I can have a clean, healthy slate for tomorrow. As a matter of fact, perhaps I should eat all the junk food I can possibly find in the house so that I can rid myself of all temptation for my clean healthy start for tomorrow because tomorrow, that fat person inside me will be trying to get back out.

My solution: Eat mindfully. Eat each little morsel of junk food aware of what I am doing. Eat slowly, savor the taste as it rolls around on my palate. After all, my mind knows that what goes in, must come out!

Three cheers for the human body's elimination function. Without it, I'd be a fat person on the outside trying to get skinny.

Chapter Eight: There Goes That Glass Again

The bird and the mice unite. I'm not paranoid, but I know they're out to get me!

Before I go on too much about what came next in my life, I need to tell you just one more thing about one of the animals in my life. As you know by now, Marty, the girls, and I, all adore dogs. It hardly matters what kind they are, we love them all. I've never had much of an affinity for cats. It's not that I don't like them, I am allergic to them, so I've had very little experience being around them. When Marty and I got married, we were very young. We were actually the first of any of our friends to get married. Most of our friends were young and didn't even have their first jobs out of school. Therefore, the wedding gifts our friends gave to us became quite creative. One of my favorites was one, from a dear friend I met freshman year in college. His gift was a letter. It was the most beautifully written letter I've ever received from anyone. It was a heartfelt letter about our friendship thus far including two premonitions: 1) that Marty and I would have a happy life together and 2) that we would always stay in touch with him. Both premonitions came true. That letter was one of the best gifts

I've ever received. I still have it. My second favorite wedding gift was from a friend who had an aviary in his backyard. He raised albino cockatiels and gave us one as a wedding present. We named her Blossom, and she was the sweetest little bird I've ever known. We'd come home from work and let her out of her cage. She would fly to us when we called her and snuggled into my neck while I sat on the couch. She had a sweet soft little chirp. In short, she was a joy to have. We never quite knew what happened, but one day upon arriving home from work, Blossom was found expired at the bottom of her cage.

It wasn't long after her loss, that Marty decided that we needed to replace her. Now if you don't know much about birds, a cockatiel stands maybe six inches tall. When we went to the pet store, Marty fell in love with a white cockatoo. It was a triton cockatoo to be exact. This bird, whom we were told was a year old and answered to the name of Elliott, stood more like twelve inches tall and cost a bloody fortune. But we had such fond memories of Blossom, and Marty was in love. So Elliott came home with us. Marty went to work the next day leaving me home alone with Eli. At first, I was just annoyed by all the seeds he threw everywhere within his reach. But then, Eli wouldn't stop screaming the entire day. I don't mean chirping loudly, I mean, screaming so loud and so long that I could feel the little hairs inside my ears vibrate. I thought I'd go deaf. By the time Marty got home, I was beside myself. I had the bird, the cage, and all that came with them, set out by the front door.

"It's the bird or me." I told Marty.

"I'm not taking the bird back," he said.

Well that shows ya just where I stood. I didn't stand very tall. That day, was thirty-three years ago. We still have Eli. Eli still screams. I still hate this animal. You could say we have a hate-hate relationship with each other that's been going on for over three decades. Eli is the only animal on the planet I have animosity towards, and I've been living with him for all this time. He's moved with us from state to state to state. He's older than my children. Why do I keep him," you might ask? I keep him because Marty loves him. I keep him because I love Marty. But I can tell you without a shadow of a doubt that I hope when my time comes to die, that I die first, before Marty, because if Marty should go before me, that bird will be out of the house before I call the undertaker. But that's how much I love my husband.

Thus Marty had Eli's love, I had Marty's love, and we both loved our two dogs. Life was going smoothly for quite a while there. I was working. Marty had a good job. The girls were in college. We had a nice house. Basically, we had the American dream. We had the stuff and the love. I'd hit the lottery of life. But remember 2008? Remember the mortgage crisis? Yep, we got stuck right smack in the middle of it all. It didn't hit us until 2010, but when it did, it sucked the liquid back out of the glass. The financial trouble started when my cancer kept coming back in rapid succession. I was struggling to resuscitate myself from one, when six months later, the cancer hit again. By the third time, I wasn't getting back to work too quickly, and my employer's patience finally ran out. My company forced me to go out of work and onto disability. Then Marty's company went out of business. The next set of essays will explain a bit about what transpired.

I'm here to tell you though, that my grateful meter went up to a very high level when it was all said and done. I knew this when my biggest problems were cleaning up after Eli's seed throwing, and my new group of rodent friends. You see, it may take some doing, but rodents are a solvable problem. It's all perspective. I also try to explain a bit about why you haven't much heard about religion playing a role in my life, and how all I ever needed was to look at the strength in my own mom and mother-in-law, to know how to overflow once again.

The Unraveling

It's done. I did it. I could feel myself blinking as I stared at the computer screen glaring back at me. But confetti didn't start dancing across the screen, and trumpets didn't start playing a celebratory tune out of the small laptop speakers. Although I didn't feel like I thought I would, like an Iranian woman doing the happy dance to Pharrell Williams song "Happy," I did feel a shiver run through the fabric of my blouse right after I hit that "submit" button: the one that finally sent off the last of the student loan payments.

It had been a long haul. In 2008 when all the banks started failing and American's finances were unraveling, we were strong. We were both employed in good jobs that we liked, one daughter was graduating from college, and the other was successfully enjoying the conclusion of her Sophomore year. Both our parents' paid for each of us to go to college, so it was never a question that we would pay for our girls to go. We had the mortgage, the cars, the cleaning service, the gym memberships, the tuitions...until we caught up with the knotted thread of our other fellow unravelers.

When I got sick and was forced to go out on disability, we were still ok. My husband had a good job. I went on his health insurance plan. We cut back. We paid the mortgage. We made the car payment, we paid the insurance premiums, we paid the tuitions. We were ok. Yes. I kept reassuring myself. We had savings. He had a good job. We were fine.

But my husband's company was bleeding money. They decided to cut their losses, and in 2010, they closed their doors. With his company going out of business, we couldn't even get COBRA. So it was health issues, with a pre-existing condition, and very expensive health insurance, that brought us to the day we had to play the game "pay the doctor or pay the mortgage." The doctor won.

For the longest time, I couldn't discuss it with anyone. It was too embarrassing to tell anyone we were having financial problems. Family and friends would invite us out and we would decline. At first we declined to save money. Even going to visit family at their house for a meal cost money. I couldn't go empty handed, so that meant spending money to make a dish, or to bring flowers, and gas and tolls added up quickly.

Eventually, we declined because we were both just too depressed. Never leaving the walls of our home forced us to create our own prison-a prison of shame and guilt and depression.

Finally, I started to talk about it. Like sewing together the pieces of a garment, one stitch at a time, I would describe our predicament, one story at a time until I explained just how we got from the comfort of where we came from to where we were now.

I'd always wondered why people vandalized their own homes when faced with foreclosure. My feeling had always been that the bank loaned me money in good faith and that it was my duty to repay that loan with the same good faith. It wouldn't take long, before I understood. Suddenly, I became a second class citizen, a deadbeat. Corporate America didn't share in my pain. They just wanted their money. It didn't matter how much I worked with them, how riddled with shame I was, or how sick I was. All that mattered was that they weren't getting paid. It would have been bad enough having to deal with our inability to pay our mortgage after almost twenty-five years of never missing a payment. What made it all worse was the unethical manner in which the bank worked with us-against us. While I can't prove anything illegal occurred, I have mounds of proof of the astounding number of unethical things the bank did to make our situation worse. There were claims of lost paperwork, paperwork they claimed to never have received, unanswered phone calls and e-mails, false information handed out, threats, and more, all while we were making every attempt to work with them as ethically as we knew how. It is the result of all that frustration that now causes me to understand why I've heard so many stories about homeowners tearing apart their own homes in order not to leave a pristine home to a bank who has treated them with anything but respect. But I wasn't going to give them what they gave me. I left the home in mint condition when I locked the door behind me. It closed shut with a quiet click just loud enough for me to hear an echo through the walls of the empty house.

Almost eight years have passed since the start of our saga. We were the lucky ones. By sheer luck, we had a window of opportunity to sell the home outright. It sold. We paid the bank every penny we owed. For three years I did not own a home, something I had done for the previous twenty-five years. But I also no longer owed anyone anything. I had no mortgage payment. I had no car payment. I had no credit card debt, and as of today, I officially paid in full for my kids to go to college.

Before the unraveling, excitement equaled spending: going to a nice restaurant, going on a nice vacation, buying a new car. I won't say I don't enjoy those things now, I do, but excitement today looks more like the threads that hold my life together. It's not the heavy embellished stitches that occasionally accent my life that make it exciting. It's the even ones: the ones that go in and out, in and out slowly piecing things back together that let me stand tall and feel proud to see my kids start life debt free and without any dangling threads to kink up their lives. Today, excitement equals pushing a submit button on the computer and seeing the number zero for account balance-no confetti, no trumpets, no happy dance.

Of Mice and Ice

At 91, Bubby, "the badass grandma of the family," confirms the story to be true that she once found a mouse in her house. At the time, there was a live-in maid, a husband, and any one of five children she could have called upon to hear her scream and to assist her in the prompt removal of the intruder. But no scream ensued, and no request for assistance was made. She grabbed a bucket and a broom. She cornered the critter and swept it up into the bucket. She then approached the kitchen sink and proceeded to fill the bucket with water. Continuing on her mission, she then grabbed the mouse with her bare hands, held it under the water until she was sure it drowned, drained the bucket, placed the mouse in the trash, and called it a day.

That was my mother-in-law: tough, independent, and full of grit.

And then there's me. I grew up mostly in Texas and partly in The Cayman Islands. To me, if the temperature doesn't start with the number seven, eight, or nine, it's too damn cold. Ok, if it starts with a six and I'm in direct sun with a sweater on, that's acceptable. Where I hale from we got a once a year ice storm. You stayed home, toasted marshmallows by the crackling fire, made hot chocolate, and by the next day you got in your muddy car, and went back to work. You enjoyed your one winter day per year and life went on. Also being from Texas, I've seen my share of roaches the size of small dinosaurs and tarantulas hanging on the edge of the toll takers change basket, enough times that it doesn't shock me. And in the Caymans' if you haven't enjoyed a beach sunset by being eaten alive by mosquitoes then you are lying and you've never really been there. So I know to stay home in bad weather, and not to scream at the sight of creepy crawly things.

Today, snow fell upon my suburban Philly home. I stayed indoors while it proceeded with its dumpage. But by two o'clock the snow stopped, and I came to the realization that I was going to have to finally, after all these years, shovel the driveway-no maid, no husband home from work, no children home for a visit. So I set out to get my rarely worn snow gloves, and snow boots from our spare room.

The other thing we keep in the spare room is my husband's cockatoo. I say he's my husband's bird because I claim no ownership of him whatsoever. As a matter of fact, I've called my husband at least once a month for the past thirty-three years of his ownership of the thing to tell him that I am putting a bird in the oven for dinner. It is the bird's utter fortune that the grocery stores give us a free turkey every year for Thanksgiving. Elliott sits in our spare room in his cage and puts his white dander all over the surface of everything so that I have to dust in there almost as often as I have to inhale. He gets a fresh bowl of seeds and nuts daily.

Later, my daughter came to visit for the weekend. She was in dire need of mommy love and rest. After dusting, of course, I put her in the spare room to sleep. Eli, lucky me, slept in our room with us. By morning, my daughter was distraught. She hadn't slept a wink. Something was scratching around her room all night and kept her up. Yep, we had a mouse in the house. My first reaction was to call my husband, but he doesn't have his mother's grit. Neither do I. I didn't make a bee line for the bucket and the broom. I did set traps, and the varmint was caught and tossed in a day. Back to the spare room I went to dust and vacuum out seeds, and nuts, and mouse droppings. Incident over- or so I thought.

I still had to shovel. I texted my husband to tell him that the shoveling was about to commence. As I was going into the spare room to get my supplies, I heard a knock at my door. It was the young man who raked my leaves last month offering to shovel. I forced myself to say no. I again texted my husband to tell him of the boy's offer, and that I declined. He texted back telling me I was crazy and to hunt the kid down and pay him twenty bucks. But I needed this. I needed to have some future vindication in my back pocket for the next time he complained about mowing the lawn. I was determined to face the snow, and the wind, and the temperature that started with some number way smaller than six. To the spare room I went to put on the gloves and the boots. One foot went into one boot. The other foot went into the other. No, the other foot tried to go into the other. What? What's going on? The other boot was filled with seeds, nuts, and a very appealing smattering of mouse droppings. It seems I cleaned all around and under, but not inside. I didn't scream. I didn't call for backup. I emptied the boot, placed it on my foot, and went outside to shovel snow all by myself for the very first time in my life. I texted my husband once again.

"Good thing ur mother taught me about mice as I step into a snow boot filled with bird seeds and droppings."

His response was priceless:

"Nice place to live. Cheap rent."

My response:

"Agreed."

I may not ever live up to my mother-in-law's reputation as a bad ass Grandma, but I can say that after mice and ice, I do have at least a little of her grit.

Just Breathe

Everything seems to piss me off lately. It started with the cable company. Every month, my bill kept getting higher and higher, yet I had done nothing different from one month to the next. When I called them, they explained to me that the amount I was paying when I first signed up with them was an introductory rate that had ended. So I asked what I thought was a logical question: "why didn't it just go up once then, and stay the same after that?" She spoke with a heavy accent, but I could swear I could hear her say it was because they felt like it.

Then I was pissed because my doctor wanted to order me orthotics. Now it's bad enough that I was old enough to need orthotics, but I was also unemployed at the time and a large durable goods purchase was not conducive to keeping to my budget. I informed the doctor's office that I would only order the orthotics if they could confirm that they were covered by my insurance. They called a few days later to tell me that they were covered and I approved the order. A year later, I got the bill after the insurance company denied the claim.

My next anger management challenge came when we went on our first vacation in years. We got to the airport with our printed confirmations only to find out that the airlines had overbooked the flight. "Not to worry," they said, "we can confirm that one of you will be on the plane." I really don't recall the last time I heard of a couple celebrating their anniversary vacation in separate parts of the world.

So I remind myself to breathe. Just breathe.

The great thing about life is that you can always make an attitude correction. I'm here to report to you that I now have a one-year price guarantee in writing from the cable company. After submitting the confirmation number to the insurance company and proving their pre-approval, I finally got the orthotics covered, and we finally ended up going on an amazing vacation with both of us in the same place at the same time.

But even better, are all the little things that happened to me lately. I needed onions at the grocery store this week. Wouldn't you know they were on sale! I got stuck in a snow embankment and three separate men stopped to help me. In five minutes, I was on my way! I left my coupon at home, and a woman gave me hers on her way out the door. My daughter chose to take me out to dinner on a Saturday night. My mother called just to hear my voice. My belly is full and my house is warm. Thank God for the little things.

Now breathe.

Of Mice and Ice: The Sequel

I bought some new towels last month and stored them in our guest bedroom drawer with our spare blankets. Now this would not be newsworthy information to you if I didn't also have to report that one of these new towels has a big fat whole in it. I'm embarrassed to tell you that hole was caused by an uninvited guest.

I've already written recently on the topic of mice and ice, but alas, my saga continues. Again, it happened in my spare room. I wouldn't have even known about it, if my husband hadn't crept in there in the middle of the night to seek refuge from my snoring. He was sound asleep in peaceful quiet bliss, when I had to get up to relieve my senior bladder at three a.m. It was then that I saw him on top of the bedspread without any covers. Upon opening the dresser drawer to pull out a blanket for him, I discovered my new towels were covered in nuts and seeds carried there by said uninvited guest or guests. I do not yet know if the towel feast was enjoyed alone or if there was a party, but I can tell you that I'm getting a complex because I wasn't invited.

This is really getting most embarrassing. I don't recall by mother ever being uninvited to the social event of the century. I don't recall my mother ever having mice in our house growing up. She kept a clean home. I believe I keep a clean home too. So what gives?

Could it be my husband's feathered friend's leftovers are too much for the critters to pass up? Could it be that winter has just been too long and they need a warm refuge? Maybe I'm just such an amazing hostess that they come from miles around just to visit.

Perhaps I should be thanking them because I saved a lot of money not having to send out save the date notices and formal invitations. The cost of postage just went up again ya know.

I'm an Atheist Jew and a Good Christian

I'm an atheist Jew and a good Christian. Please allow me to explain myself. I was raised as a reform Jew. In our household, this meant we were "one" Jews. One day of eight was celebrated for Passover, one of eight for Chanukah, and one time a year we went to High Holiday services.

When I was a little girl, I remember asking my dad if he believed in God. He told me that as a doctor he felt he had to believe in God because he witnessed the miracle of self-healing on a daily basis. He told me that he couldn't believe that the intricacies of the human body just occurred by accident. From that day forward, I believed in God.

When I went off to college, I lived in a Jewish dorm and dated only Jewish boys. I met and married a Jewish man. When I began to raise children, I felt that I needed more "Jewishness" in the home. So we joined a synagogue, sent the children to religious school, and began to keep the Sabbath. We might have piano lessons and sports six nights a week, but on Friday night, our dinner table was adorned with a white tablecloth, Shabbat candles, my husband's Kiddush cup, and a challah. We recited prayers, and the best meal of the week was enjoyed. Most importantly, I began to volunteer. To me, teaching my girls by example was the very best way to teach. I wanted them to know the importance of empathy and compassion, and I wanted them to know how to appreciate what they had. We lived in the south where there was a much smaller population of Jews per capita then there is here in the Northeast. With all my good deeds, it was on more than one occasion that my children would hear someone tell me what a good Christian I was for the work that I was doing. It was on more than one occasion that the teller, knew I was a Jew. But their meaning was understood, and my example for my children was still instilled.

Over the years, life's challenges began to take their toll. Without a doubt, the good in my life has well outweighed the bad, but the bad has left its mark. Too many times I listened to the evening news to hear a near miss victim state that it was "by the grace of God" that their home was still standing or that their loved ones were still alive. I began to wonder, did God not grace their neighbor, the one who lost their home and their loved ones? Yes, I became cynical. I began to have my doubts in God.

9/11 was the formal day I lost all faith in God. It wasn't just that my own husband was right in the thick of it that day. It wasn't just that 3000 of my fellow American's lost their lives that day. I think it was the fact that the terrorists did it in the name of God. Really? God wanted them to murder thousands of innocent people to ensure he had their faith? I just couldn't buy it. God walked out the door for me that day. He's never walked back in.

Sometimes, I feel badly about being a non-believer. Sometimes, I'm embarrassed to tell people that I don't believe in God. I have to admit that it made me feel just a little better when my ninety-year-old mother-in-law, who kept kosher all her life, finally went to Ruth's Chris to enjoy a steak and a baked potato with sour cream on it stating that if God wanted to send her to hell for ninety years of keeping kosher and one sinful meal, then so be it.

I continue to volunteer for all kinds of things. I continue to live a life with what I believe to be a good moral compass. I continue to celebrate the food, family, and festivities of Jewish holidays. I still have people tell me that I'm a good Christian. I just do it all now, while being an atheist.

Of Mice and Ice: The Hopeful Conclusion

Every year since my kids were very young, I've decorated the house for each of the different holidays. In September, you will find the walls of my home donning red, white, and blue for Labor Day. In October, you'll find orange and black, pumpkins, and ghosts. So you'll understand when I tell you that last week, I broke out the Thanksgiving decorations bin. Inside, I found a surprise. Upon opening the bin, I discovered a large mass of dust. When I turned the bin upside down, I discovered that my Thanksgiving wreath was underneath all the dust. But it wasn't exactly my Thanksgiving wreath. It was what was left of my Thanksgiving wreath after "someone" got hold of it. You see each fall, as we came and went through the front door of our home, we would get pummeled with acorns falling from our large oak tree. One year, I decided to make use of the acorns by collecting a bin of them and gluing them to a straw wreath. With a few finishing touches of mini Indian corn and a bow, I had myself a homemade Thanksgiving wreath for years to come...or so I thought. We've since moved away from that home, but I still have the same bins filled with holiday decorations for every month of the year. Although we called in the big guns last year, the professional rodent removers, it seems we didn't call them in before our uninvited guests had a Thanksgiving feast of their own because this year, my lovely wreath is not quite so lovely. The dust was the pulverized remains of the inside of the acorns and the kernels of Indian corn. Since I no longer have access to free acorns, this year, we'll just have to suffer through a skeleton wreath donning our front door.

A Beautiful Table

Her hands shook as I sat across the table from her watching her sip from her half cup of coffee. I had seen her only a few months earlier, but the Parkinson's had gotten worse since I was last there to visit. Part of the problem was that she was due to have brain surgery to improve the symptoms, and she was told to go off her meds pre-surgery.

I watched those hands...the ones that held me when I was little, the ones that rubbed away the cold from my own hands to keep me warm, the ones that always set the most beautiful table for company. My mom has many talents, but one of her very best was setting an amazing table. Nowadays, this is almost a lost art. But before the Parkinson's started, even only four or five years ago, you could find my mom setting the table.

First she'd choose the proper tablecloth from her collection of thirty or more embroidered linens. Sometimes she would even choose a colored fabric to peek through the lace from underneath. Then she would decide which china to use, which crystal, which silver. These choices always had to carefully compliment the linen as well as the food to be served. Then she would put the final touches on her table by choosing the manner in which to fold the napkins, the color of the candlesticks, the choice in candelabra, and finally, the flowers.

Both my parents loved to entertain. My dad would always make sure the liquor cabinet was stocked and he would sometimes whip up a special drink in the blender or even create a signature salad to go with the meal for the impending company, but it was always mom who set the dinner table and fussed over the main menu. You could see the twinkle in dad's eyes when she was done...just before the company arrived. He would step back and admire the beauty of her table. It was never the same setting, and it was always a work of art.

But over the last several years, mom's shaking prevented her from almost any dexterity in the kitchen, and she rightly began to fear setting a table with all her beautiful supplies because the possibility of dropping her beloved china plates or her fine crystal was all too probable. My parents still insisted on entertaining. When their friends would invite them over, they were served pre-made hors d'oeuvres or make-your-own ice cream. But they still insisted on inviting their friends to full blown dinner parties with multiple course meals and mom's beautiful table. Only now, it was dad doing the cooking, and it was dad setting the table. Mom would still direct, but I know she missed doing it herself. Not once, not a single time, did I hear her complain.

So now, the day before her surgery, it didn't surprise me that she didn't fear the impending brain surgery. She's always been brave when fear has faced her. The thing that upset her the most, was her hair appointment. She had to get her head shaved. But my dad had a surprise in store for her. When he picked me up at the airport, he drove me straight to the beauty salon. The beautician was stalling, waiting not only for us to arrive, but for the guitarist my dad had hired to serenade mom at her most vulnerable time. We made it into a celebration, "the celebration of the shaving of the head," and we did celebrate. We sang, and we hugged, and we sang some more, all right there in the beauty salon. Watching my parents love for one another brought tears to my eyes. They've been married for over sixty years. There is nothing they won't do for one another. What an amazing idea my dad had. I hope that it distracted her just enough to look into his eyes and see his love instead of looking into the mirror to see the loss of her hair, because on that day, she lost very little, and gained all the more love and respect from those around her. I didn't think it was possible for me to love her or my dad any more than I already did, but seeing them together, vulnerable, in that beauty salon, trying to celebrate life, made me remember what heroes they both are for standing up and rising to the occasion with dignity and love.

That night, the night before the surgery, I watched my mom, my hero, as she shuffled across the hallway with her Parkinson's gate. She kissed me good night with her face missing the compassionate expression it always had because the disease robbed it from her. Before I kissed her back, I wished upon her all the love and tenderness she'd shared with me to go right back into her. I told her that I hoped, of course, that the next day's surgery would be successful and would allow her to once again whip up her gourmet meals and set her beautiful table. But she surprised me. She said that now that dad had taken over the kitchen, it was just fine with her to let him do all the work. My mother's no dummy. But it was no surprise, when she admitted that she would love to set another table.

Before I closed my eyes that night, I had to bring my mind back to the rest of my life back at home. My daughter was about to leave her company to move on to a new job. The company she was working for went by the name of "Gotham." So I sent her a quick text and told her I wished her luck in her last week in Gotham City and that I hoped she had a chance to meet Batman while she was there. It was my attempt at a little stupid humor to relieve my stress. But she one upped me with her response. She texted me back the following:

"Mom, I don't know how to tell you this, but I *am* Batman."

Oh how I laughed. But you know what? She's right, she is a superhero. She learned how to be one straight from her grandmother. All she had to do was watch her grandmother set a beautiful table to learn.

Chapter Nine: How'd I Get Old?

Wouldn't you get lost in this?   Just give it a good whack, right on top!

I went to the mall with Marty the other day. While I stopped in a store to try something on, he went to grab a coffee. Upon his return, I was still back in the dressing room. He asked the sales clerk to please let me know that he was back and waiting for me. She did come back to speak with me. She told me that my son was waiting in the store for me. My son! Are you kidding me? Marty and I are only a few months apart in age and have been married for over thirty years. Now I know he's a handsome guy, and I'm not winning any beauty contests, but really? I wasn't sure if I should be insulted because I'm in my fifties and must have looked to her as if I was in my seventies, or if I should consider it a compliment since I'm obviously attractive enough to be a cougar who's got a young thing to wait on me.

So between that and my AARP card, I guess I got old. I'm tech savvy, but I'm not. I adapt, but I don't. I forget what I remember, and I remember what I forget.

137

Technology

(This next essays uses a term called the "mix master." If you are not from Texas, you need to know that a mix master, aside from being a kitchen aide, is also what we call the huge highway entrances that loop up and over other highways.)

Oh God. I'm in the mix master. The wire beaters are like the tentacles from a deep sea creature. They're wrapping themselves around my hands forcing me to tighten my grip on the steering wheel. Maybe my white knuckled hands will grip it tightly enough that I rip it right off its axis and force the car to drive in the right direction. Now I'm hysterical. It's that crazy woman on the highway hysterical. I see my fellow Texas drivers evacuating the area. I've seen it before. It's the only time I ever see them parting the hairs of the highway to leave bald spots between me and the other cars. I'm lost.

Again.

I find an exit, a gas station, and a phone. I call my husband. I tell him I'm by that four story building with the blue stripe across the top. I tell him that across the street there's a Texaco station next to a McDonald's. He's not recognizing the landmarks I'm giving him. I'm shouting into the phone. "I'm by the place we had lunch that day. You know, the one with the good salads." My voice is shaky and my hands smell like the metal from the keys that have been melting in my sweaty palms. "Just tell me how to get home. Why can't you just tell me how to get home?" He asks me to go find another person, any other human being, and ask them to come to the phone to tell him where I am.

That was me. That was fifteen years ago, and twenty years ago, and thirty years ago. I have spacial dyslexia. Now admittedly this is a term I coined out of my own need to give credibility to my lifelong malady, but it seems a concise term to explain my legitimate handicap. When I was sixteen, I got lost going to the DMV to get my first driver's license. I've been getting lost ever since.

In school, algebra was a breeze. If you know the formula, you know how to solve the equation. Trigonometry, that was another story. "Picture the triangle on a plane in space," the teacher would say. That's like telling a woman to dry her pee in a public stall without the use of toilet paper. It can be done, but it will take a lot of time and a lot of patience.

I used to carry those spiral bound laminated maps of the entire city displaying how to get from one neighborhood to the next, but I lacked the ability to read the maps. They just collected my sweat drippings when I tried to read them.

But then a miracle came along. The internet was invented. I punched in how to get from home to my first destination, from my first to my second, to my third, and back home. I had turn by turn directions every day before I left my front door. This worked well for me until the day came in which my need to get to point "B" was canceled. I had to figure out how to get from point "A" to point "C". When people said you can't get there from here, I took it literally.

Another miracle came along: GPS. I was the first bozo standing in line to plunk down $700 of my hard-earned money to purchase the first generation of one of these contraptions. I don't mind when the little lady in the box tells me "when possible, make a legal U-turn". I may have missed the turn, but at least now I know I missed it thirty seconds after I missed it. All I have to do is make a "legal U-turn" and I'm home free. Don't ask me about the day last month when my old GPS died on me in the middle of a busy day. Ok, you can ask me. I felt that crazy woman on the highway hysteria welling up in my chest. I pulled over and called my husband in that shaky voice of the late last century. Then I used my smart phone to jump start me home.

The very next day, I exuberantly plunked down $70 for my brand new GPS with all the bells and whistles. When she chimes, it sounds like laughter to me. Sometimes, when there's a road block, she doesn't know it's there. So she takes me around in a circle making me end up right back where I started, in front of the same road block. I laugh at myself for following her. Then I make a turn away from the road block. I ignore her instructions for a bit, then she reroutes herself and gets me back on the path to my destination. She makes me chuckle when she repeats herself and says "rerouting, rerouting." I like that she makes me laugh because if she wasn't rerouting, I'd be reverting, back to the days of being lost and hysterical. I had to pull off the road right after I got my newest version of her so that I could once again be hysterical. But this time, it was the funny ha ha kind of hysterical.

In 2018, some have resolved to limit their use of technology. I will not be limiting mine.

Learning To Adapt

It started about a year ago, when I first noticed that words I wanted to use just wouldn't come to me. I knew the context in which I wanted to use them. I knew the definition. I just couldn't think of the damn word. I've never had a great memory, but this was frustrating. It was also a little scary. Was I getting the beginnings of Alzheimer's? But like everything else in life, I learned to cope.

I'll admit, that I was a latecomer when it came to using a smart phone. Although first in line to ditch my landline way back in 2004, the smart phone had no appeal to me. I just wanted to be able to make a call. Then I just wanted to text. But I certainly had my computer for everything else. A few years ago, when my cell phone died, I went to the store and actually used the following words to describe to the salesman what I wanted.

"Can you just sell me the cheapest old lady phone? I don't need all the bells and whistles, I just want to be able to make calls and send a text now and then."

Seriously, I used the words, "sell me the cheapest old lady phone." As it happens, the cheap old lady phone was $35, not including service of course. The previous years' iPhone, was .99 cents. Being the frugal woman that I am, I took the iPhone home with me. Which brings me to the point of the story: how I learned to adapt.

Now when that word just won't come to me, I Google the thesaurus, and voila, success. I learned to adapt. In a crowd of people some of whom are acquaintances, and some of whom I've never met, I can't always remember which is which. Therefore, I use the following catch phrase:

"Nice to see you."

This way, if I've already met them-no problem. If I am meeting them for the first time-no problem. I've learned to adapt.

Introductions can get a little trickier, but I've got an adaptation for that one too. When introducing someone who's name I simply cannot remember to someone I've known for a long time, I simply introduce my old friend by name to the other party. Etiquette wise, it's not exactly proper, but somehow, I'm vain enough that I'd rather look ignorant of formal manners than appear missing a few marbles. I pick my battles, and vanity wins. I've learned to adapt.

I even took a class once on remembering people's names. I know you've heard of these classes before. They instruct you to remember a new name by

a) repeating it upon first hearing it, and

b) associating it with something else.

What the twenty something instructor didn't say was how to remember the name long enough to repeat it, and how to remember the association! But that twenty something instructor's got nothin' on me because me, well I've learned to adapt.

I must say, I'm actually quite proud of myself for my preparations for the eventuality of hearing loss. My dad just got his first hearing aids. He was most concerned with either getting the tiny one that goes into your ear canal or at the very least, the kind that goes behind the ear in grey so that it blends in with his silver hair. Not me, when I have to take the plunge I'm getting the biggest boldest blackest one I can find. That way, when people see it, they'll think I'm really hip because they'll think it's my blue tooth. How many hip seniors do you know who can't live without their blue tooth? I've learned to adapt to that one, and I don't even need it yet. Yea me!

As for height shrinkage, I've just about covered that one too. I've learned to sew, so hemming will be a cinch, and let's face it, by the time I have to face being altitude-challenged, there'll be an app for that.

Technology 2.0

I have a love-hate relationship with technology. I previously wrote about my malady of spacial dyslexia and how I have vowed to never give up my GPS. But things are a little different when it comes to all other technical devices. I'm not paranoid, but they're all out to get me.

Personally, I think that all people over the age of fifty who know how to navigate a mouse, use a keyboard, and surf the net, should win a Noble Peace Prize for the ability to communicate with the younger generation. I thought I was pretty tech savvy, for a woman of my advanced years, for the sheer reason that I can't live without e-mail, I use a Kindle, I own and use a smartphone, I text regularly, and I have my own Facebook page. I was wrong.

I don't Snapchat or Instagram. I tried to pin things on Pinterest but the safety pin got stuck and wouldn't budge. I was ok with the world without these things. I was comfortable with my laptop software, my smartphone, and my Kindle.

But when the Kindle broke, I did a happy dance. Now I can go back to the library for free and get a glue high every time I crack a new book. There's just nothing better than taking a whiff of that hypnotic euphoria. I was at peace with the laptop until the battery decided to die a long and painful death. I knew enough to regularly back up my computer, but I still don't know how to use my external hard drive. Trying to save things in the "cloud" was creating too much fog in my brain. I was forced to buy a new computer.

Since I don't do any gaming, and don't need much in the way of speed or storage space, I purchased an inexpensive laptop with the new Windows 8. Now I was just fine with Windows 7 and Vista, but Windows 8 is a nightmare. What little tech knowledge I did have went right out that eighth window. When I finally figured out how to use it "the old way" from my desktop, I thought I'd do the happy dance yet again, but it was a very short dance, because I found out that all my old programs no longer worked on Windows 8. After spending more money buying all the upgrades to all the programs I needed, I was in even more of a quandary. Now I had to actually learn to use all that new software. The manuals, that I printed off to read, are collecting dust bunnies on the shelf with the broken Kindle.

I accepted my fate in stride until last week when my phone kept demanding that I upgrade to the latest version. "No," I said emphatically. "NO, I will not do it! I like my old version, the one I know how to use!" But wouldn't you know, it made me do it? It actually forced me to download the upgrade. It actually gave me warnings saying that I could only use it three more times before I had to upgrade. I'm not lying. Of course, I could have anticipated the outcome. My apps are gone, and every time I text my husband, he tells me he's getting messages from me from the clouds. I didn't realize my last trip out of state took me that far. I thought I was only going to Jersey.

They say you can't teach an old dog new tricks. I say you can. I just have a finite amount of space in my storage drive to learn.

Senior Brain Freeze

We'd pile into the car and then sit in the garage. Then she'd ask us the question. " Would one of you please go get me the thing-a-ma-jig? It's in the what-cha-ma-call-it on the little do-hickey?" That was my mom. We were supposed to decipher what she meant. Then dad would remind her that they were on her head and we could go forth into the land of errands.

It never made sense to me that mom couldn't quite speak in English. She was second generation native born American and spoke with no accent, yet she could never get every word she meant out into open air.

Last week, it finally clicked. I went to the lady's room in my office building. I went there with the obvious mission ahead. But then I stood at the threshold of the door trying to remember the cockamamie code to punch into the door to unlock the precious toilets inside. I've been working in the same building for over a year. The combination to the lock has never once changed. Yet I simply could not remember the code. I stood there for a moment hoping perhaps that some other, younger, woman would happen by to let me in, but I had no such luck. I turned around, went back to my office, and back to my desk. I was much too embarrassed to ask one of my coworkers for the combination. Had they just changed the code, I would have had no problem asking someone to remind me of the new combination of numbers for the privilege of entry into the lady's room. Had I been new to the building, I would have had no problem asking for a reminder. But alas, it was neither of these. It was a senior moment.

Fortunately for me, I was not desperate at the time. I resumed work, and thirty minutes later, I remembered the code and went forth into blissful relief.

So now, mom, I understand what only dad could understand when you wanted someone to get the thing-a-ma-jig for you. I want someone to get one for me too if I can only just remember what it is.

Username and Password

There are times today when I feel like an immigrant from another country. There's an old joke about a guy who comes to this country speaking very little English. Every day, he goes to the same diner and orders apple pie and coffee. He doesn't know enough of the language to order anything else. One day, he meets a man who teaches him how to order a ham and cheese sandwich. Excitedly, he goes to the diner to order his new and long awaited meal when the waitress asks him if he wants his sandwich on white or rye. Frustrated and confused, he finally reverts back to ordering his apple pie and coffee.

I feel for this fictitious man every time I get on my computer. Each time I log on, it's like traveling to a foreign country. It's an adventure that includes surfing, hard drives, and the need for more memory. Every day, I sit in front of my same computer, and every day I plug in my same username and password. They tell me not to do this. They tell me to use different names and passwords for different programs. But they also tell me that I can't write them down and keep them next to my computer. So the same one it is. I told you that the day I needed a new computer I went out and bought one with the latest Windows 8. As soon as I got home and turned the thing on, it asked me to set-up my username and password. So I tried to use something new while the youth in my life explained to me how to use the new-fangled apps on my computer. All was well until I tried to find the start menu to locate the program I needed to use and all hell broke loose. When I finally found the program, I couldn't remember the new username and password.

After picking up my laptop from the neighbor's yard and cleaning up the glass from the broken window I threw it out of, I rebooted the computer, and reset it to my old username and password. All is right again in my own country where I speak the language.

Stupid Thing

It used to be that I was smart and all the inanimate objects around me were stupid. I could use and abuse these objects, and no matter what, I was smart, and they were stupid.

Take TV's for example. In ancient times, I could plug in my TV, turn the "on" button, and voila! I had TV. I was smart enough to know that if I wanted to watch TV, all I had to do was plug the thing in and turn it on. Once in a while, the TV might stop working properly. The usual problem was something we called horizontal or vertical hold. Stupid TV. Abuse from an intelligent human, such as myself, usually solved the problem. I would just give the stupid thing a good bang on the top, and I'd be back in business.

Playing music is another perfect example of my personal genius vs. the stupidity of an inanimate object. I used to take a stack of these old fashioned things we called record albums. I would put several on a spindle on a record player and enjoy listening to my favorite tunes. Once in a while, the record player would misbehave by getting stuck. It would play the same part of the song over and over again. Stupid record player. I'd pick up the thing on the player we called the arm, blow on the needle it held really hard, and place it back down on the record. Success. My intelligence knew no bounds.

But nowadays, everything seems to be reversed. Now it is the objects that are smart, and I am the stupid one. I know you'll understand what I mean if you try to plug in a new TV today. First of all, they are "smart" TV's. They come with their own diplomas and make you feel stupid just trying to figure out what to plug in where. I swear my new smart TV doesn't even have an "on" button anywhere on it. Its slimness causes me grief in several different ways. First, it's so skinny that there is nothing to bang on when it doesn't work right. It's so thin that it has no rabbit ears to hear me when I try to call it stupid, and it has the nerve to be skinnier than I am. It's less than a year old and it has no baby fat to be found anywhere!

As for playing music, this is now a job for my "smart" phone. It's smart enough to know what music I like, but again, if it doesn't work the way I want it to, it has absolutely no arms for me to blow on. All the time now, I see people talking on their phones when it looks like they're talking to themselves, but no one calls them crazy, and no one calls their phone stupid. They call me stupid because I'm the only one that walks around blowing on mine trying to get the right song to come out.

Ah, but I do still have my way of getting revenge on these new "smart" objects. You see, back in ancient times, I still had the man: the repairman. I would call the repairman when there was a problem, and he would fix the object for me. In turn, the object would behave for a while and be grateful that I took the time and expense to have it repaired. Today, the man doesn't exist. No one calls anyone to fix a broken TV or a broken phone. NO! If they misbehave, they end up in the dump only to be replaced by a newer, cheaper, better version. Who's the smart one now?

The Good Old Days

I thought I was middle-aged. But I've been in possession of an AARP card for seven years now so maybe that makes me an official senior citizen. I can clearly recall when my parents would tell us all about the good old days. They would tell us that penny candy meant that you got a fist full of candy for a penny. They would tell us that movies were five cents, and that included a double feature. They would tell how they bought their first house, the beautiful house I grew up in, for $30,000. And I remember thinking, "God, they're so old."

Well here I stand today, fifty-seven-years-old, and I can remember when I first started driving, and I could fill my tank for seven bucks. I remember pay phones, not the portable devices we now carry in our pockets, but the one's that cost a dime to make a call from the inside of a little standing box. And then I remember the big things and the little things. We had big hair, big speakers for our stereos, big platform shoes, and big dreams. We had tiny transistor radios, tiny TV screens, and a tiny choice of channels to surf.

My dad made his living as a plastic surgeon. Back then, they were plastic surgeons, not cosmetic surgeons. They might lift you here and tuck you there, but they also built you a new ear when you were born with none, and made you a new face after the old one went through the front windshield. I remember vacations to a little place in the late 70's called Grand Cayman Island. There was a seven-mile stretch of beach there with only one hotel on it. There were no Ritz Carlton's, no TV's, and very few phones. And I remember go-go boots, the wet look, and bare midriff halter tops. Please God, don't bring back the bare midriff halter tops. I can't bear the thought of walking into my local Wal-Mart only to find some woman's bra strap, in hot pink, hanging uncovered on her shoulder and all her muffin top fat hanging out of her middle.

But then, so many things are really still the same. Back then, we wore black horn rimmed glasses. Today, we don't call them horn rimmed, but the fashion is still big, black, and plastic. Back then, we wore pedal pushers, today, we call them crop pants, but they're still pants that just don't make it down to your toes. The Who can still jam, Springsteen still draws a crowd, and yes, we still have big dreams.

Some things have changed for the worse, some for the better, and some have just stayed the same. I really have no desire to go back to my youth and relive the good old days. I was naive, and insecure, and limited in wisdom. I like it just where I am.

A fist full of candy is now around a buck fifty. A single feature film is now $12, and that house I grew up in can now be found online and valued at $350,000. But of course our salaries are higher and both sexes work, so who's to say that the value is all that much different.

There's just one thing, one little thing, that I really miss about the good old days. I want to go on vacation. I want to go back to Grand Cayman Island. But I want to go back in 1978. I want to go there without all the big hotels and the tourist shops. I want to go back to no TV's when I could only hear the sound of the ocean. So I need to have a little talk with the future. I need to tell it to please invent an airplane that will take me there. Take me back to Grand Cayman in 1978 because apparently, I'm a senior citizen now and that would take me back to the good old days.

They Were Old

Why is it that no matter how old you are, you're never old? You may feel old. You may complain about your aches and pains. You may even venture to look in the mirror and admit to seeing wrinkles around your eyes. If it's a full length mirror, you might go so far as to admit that some things have shifted, and the things that are supposed to go north are now going south. But it's someone else who is actually old.

In my twenties, I'd looked at women in their thirties. They stopped wearing heels. They wore kid stained shirts and drove minivans. They were old.

In my thirties, when I wore flats, stained shirts, and drove a minivan, I'd look at women in their forties. They wore glasses. They died their hair, and they were a little overweight. They were old.

In my forties, when I started wearing glasses, dying my hair, and found myself gaining weight, I'd look at women in their fifties. They stopped caring what other people thought. They made decisions on what to do, or not do, about their drooping eyes and their newfound jowls. They were old.

Now that I'm in my fifties, I try not to care what other people think. I mostly succeed. I've made my peace with my drooping eyes and my newfound jowls. But I'm still not old.

I hope I will enjoy experiencing my sixties, seventies, and beyond. I peeked into my future when my parents, told me all about all the eighty-year-old people on their recent cruise to Hawaii. They told me they all had scooters. The people on the ship, they said, they were old.

A Very Special Trip

This is the best trip ever! We get to the Airport in record time. We pull up curbside to find a friendly skycap waiting for us. He's got on one of those navy blue flat topped hats with the shiny patent leather brim-his name embroidered over the pocket of his starched shirt. He lifts our bags, two for each of us, and carts them away for a dollar tip. We're greeted at the counter by a ticket agent with a warm inviting smile. It's the kind of smile that's accompanied by a glance up at us acknowledging her gratitude for our presence. The skycap brings her our bags. She checks them, gives us claim checks, and doesn't ask us for any further payment. She hands us our boarding passes, thanks us, and directs us to our gate.

We glance down at the boarding passes with our seat assignments on them. Awesome. Two of us have the requested window seats, and two of us have the requested aisle seats. Since we have nothing to carry but our small purses, we easily walk to the gate in five minutes and hand our boarding passes to the agent at the desk. She looks so pretty. Her perfect size eight body fits smartly into her airline uniform. She too shines that now familiar grin our way, the one with the glance up and the gratitude. She hands back the passes and tells us it will only be a few minutes until we're ready to board.

I feel like an elite princess from a foreign land as we're escorted to our seats. We're sitting two and two across the aisle from one another. There is no one in either middle seat.

After take-off, we're offered a steaming, scented wash cloth to refresh ourselves and a free warm breakfast. We have our choice of an omelet or pancakes. We carefully unwrap the shiny flatware from its tightly wrapped white linen napkin. I place the napkin in my lap to protect my outfit from the possibility of a syrup mishap.

This is such an extraordinary experience that I want to savor every moment. Who gets to do this? Who gets treated like such royalty? I want to take this feeling and shrink it down to the size of a pill so it will fit in my purse. If I can just do that, then I can take it out at my whim, swallow it whole, and fall down the rabbit hole to feel like this again and again.

Our food trays are removed and we're provided with a deck of cards with the airline logo on the box. We're told we can keep the cards when we leave the aircraft.

After a pleasant flight, we come to a gentle landing and begin to disembark. I'm handed a metal pin with airline wings to attach to my party dress. It's the new one with the powder blue ribbon on it that ties on the side. It looks so pretty with my lace tights that slide neatly into my white patent leather Mary Janes. Mom reminds me to put my white gloves back on before we exit the plane.

That was over fifty years ago. I was six years old. It was my first plane trip. You already know how to describe my last plane trip. If you're out there and you can hear me, can you please call the sixties? I want my customer service back!

An Apple a Day

My father was a doctor. My father was always older than me. Therefore, all doctors should be older than me. They're supposed to be older and wiser. Until recently, all my doctors have always been older than me. A year ago, we moved to a new state. I had to find all new doctors. But I think the ones I found are fake doctors because they're all younger than me. Does this mean I'm now a doctor? I'm confused. I don't remember going to medical school. But then again, one of the new fake doctors did tell me to expect some natural memory loss.

Everything nowadays seems to be younger and smarter than I am. I have a four-month-old smartphone and a six-month-old smart TV. The phone knows ninety-four contact phone numbers, the time I wake up every morning, and with whom I'm supposed to meet for lunch tomorrow. The TV knows what I like to watch, when I want to watch it, and what I should watch next. I think next month it will take its first steps.

Advertisers are definitely smarter than I am. Obviously, only old people watch the evening news because every commercial is trying to sell me something that gets it up, helps keep it down, or creates a steady stream. Young people don't need these things that's why they check the news online. The online advertisers try to sell them something completely different. Instead of trying to sell them something to get it up, they try to sell them Virgin Mobile. I guess it's a device that keeps them virgins as long as they're mobile. The other big advertiser that markets to these young online newsies is a store called The Apple Store. These poor young kids haven't even gone to the store yet to buy their first apple.

I think I'll make it my new mission in life to keep this apple store in business, otherwise, these kids won't buy enough apples to keep the doctor away while they're still younger than he is.

It's a Generational Thing

I've looked into my future and it's not a pretty sight. I can fondly remember my Grandmother trying to use modern technology. When answering machines first came out and she would try to leave me a message, she would sign the message. No, really. She would talk into the phone stating the purpose of her call. When she was done, she would say one word, "Grandma," as if you'd had no idea who had been talking for the last two-minute message. To her, it was like signing a card. We used to laugh, both at her and with her over her card signing phone messages.

Skip down one generation to my mom. She's had a microwave since 1976 but she still takes a bag of frozen vegetables and puts them in a pot of water to boil on the stove. She has voicemail and she's armed with a cell phone, but I can't quite grasp why she bothers. While she has almost completely figured out how to check her voicemail messages, she hasn't quite mastered the cell phone. She never has it with her when she needs it, and if she does, it isn't charged. She gives her cell number to her friends and to her doctors so of course, they call her on it. But most of the time, she doesn't have it with her. When she does have it with her and it's charged, she doesn't hear it ring as it is buried deep down into the hallows of her purse. If she does hear it ring, she can't answer it fast enough and she misses the call anyway. Then she doesn't understand how to check her messages. So now the doctor's office called to reschedule her appointment, and she never got the message. Then she shows up for the appointment only to be disappointed. It's like an episode of "The Twilight Zone." You can't tell if she's in the pre-technology world or in the present. And don't get me started with the computer.

For her birthday this year, we decided to get her a smartphone. This was my brilliant idea. I thought it would make her life easier. Instead of trying to scroll through a directory to find her contact names, instead of trying to figure out how to send an e-mail, and instead of trying to remember a password to check her voicemail messages, all she had to do is push one button to talk to Siri, and she'd be in business. Little did I realize that even after I programmed in all her contact's names, phone numbers, and e-mails, that she would still have to be capable of pushing the one button to use Siri. God help us if the correct screen is not displayed and she has to deal with any other button/app. She can't quite grasp the fact that apps don't work like buttons, you can't "push" them to make them work. I've tried to define a "tap" vs. a "push" for her, but all was completely lost when I had forgotten all about the swoosh to enter a previously resting phone. Insert smile here to prevent utter frustration.

Then there's me. When computers first came out, I'd watch my toddlers climb up on a chair and tap and click until their little hearts were content. I thought that if they could do it, well so could I. So I sat down and taught myself the basics. When cell phones became the norm, I was one of the first to get rid of our land line. I frequently prefer e-mails and texts to phone calls, and although someone else actually set it up, I'm even a blogger. But I seem to be approaching my future more closely lately. I can hear the giggles of my daughters as I try to keep up. They laugh at me when I accidently send a group message when it's meant for only one, and they laugh at me when I think that tweeting is for birds and pinning is for seamstresses.

But I'm ok with my future as I try and will eventually fail to keep up. It's a time honored tradition created by the amazing women of my family. I will happily pass it on to my girls. Besides, eventually, they'll be my age, and their children will be laughing at them. Laugh away my beautiful girls because if I can make you and any of my future grandchildren laugh, then I've truly accomplished something for the ages.

On Menopause

You're on the rag. You're on your period. Your little friend is visiting. You have the curse. Call me crazy, but I'm the only woman I know of that's actually praying for menopause to hit. I was doing just fine until I hit the age of fifty. When I went for my annual check-up, my doctor told me that the birth control pills I'd been on for almost thirty years were no longer necessary. She said that my chances of getting pregnant were slim. My first question to her thirty something self was the following:

"Whose chances? Yours or mine?"

I was reluctant. But then I thought about having one less chemical in my body and saving money every month on my pharmaceutical bill, and I played along.

I had been on one of those pills in which you only get your period once every three months, so suddenly I had to get used to having a period every month again. The last time I lived with that, I was in my twenties. It may have been thirty years ago, but the memory of frequent bathroom breaks, cramps, and irritability monthly came flooding back right along with other things that were flooding.

I kept thinking that it would be ok, I'd hit menopause soon, and this would all be over. But so far, I've had no luck.

Then I went and did a really radical thing: I lost those eighty pounds. There are lots of great side effects related to the weight loss, but there's one really, really bad one. I'm freezing cold ALL THE TIME! When I go out with my girlfriends, and they complain about hot flashes, my jealousy thermometer rises, but my body temperature doesn't. When I see beads of sweat on their foreheads, it takes all my emotional control not to get a glass to collect them and rub their warm wetness on my goose bumps. And when they complain about never knowing when they're going to get their periods after skipping four months in a row, I ask them why they have an aversion to surprises. Please, wrap mine up with a bow and put it in my doggy bag. I'd like to take it home. I wouldn't mind a surprise. It's gotta be better than knowing exactly when I'll be cursed every single month.

It seems to me that Menopause is great. Aside from no longer being constantly cold, I would never again have to worry about wearing white pants on the wrong day of the month. I wouldn't have to carry a huge purse big enough to carry my fully stocked supply of feminine products, and I wouldn't have to wash my bed sheets between normal wash days, just because, well, you know.

And just think, no more cramps! I don't get what all the hullaballoo is all about. Bring it on. Come on menopause, I'm awaitin' for ya. I'm singing my ode to the menses gods to move swiftly because the day I became a "real woman" was decades ago. I no longer need proof. I'm quite real enough thank you. I'm ready to rid myself of the monthly beast. Is there a menopause Facebook page? Because I'm ready to put in my friend request.

Grown-ups

Remember when there were grown-ups in the world? I remember when they would always tell me of the three things that were bound to happen to me. Whatever I did, I was either going to break my neck, catch pneumonia, or poke my eye out. Then I was told not to make a face because it would freeze that way. And I certainly couldn't go swimming unless I waited at least a half an hour after I ate. The people doing all the telling were always larger than life, and somehow, it gave us comfort to believe that they were right.

There are still a few grown-ups that exist in the world. My mom is one of them. She still tells me about the three things that are going to happen to me, and I still want to believe that she's always right. But the larger than life part, well I'm not so sure about that one. She's an absolute two inches shorter than she was when I was a kid.

I'm fifty-seven-years old, but I'm still not a grown-up. I don't repeat the three things that will happen to my children, and I go for my morning swim directly after breakfast every day. But I do wish mom had been right about my face freezing that way because then I'd have a wrinkle free face to go with my aging body, and I wouldn't even have to pay for Botox to have it.

Commercials Are Changing My Life

I have an issue with commercials nowadays. The lack of jingles in today's commercials makes no sense to me. I think that maybe the advertisers are out to get me because they only had jingles when I was young and didn't need them as much as I do now. I still had a decent memory then, and I was emotionally well balanced. Back then, those jingles came in handy. They'd come in even more handy now.

I'd find myself in the middle of the grocery store trying to get my food shopping done for the week. There I was, in the lunch meat aisle trying to remember what it was we needed in the house. Oh, yes, lunch meat, I'd think to myself, but which kind was it that the kids wanted? All I'd have to do is think about the commercial, and I was home free: "my bologna has a first name it's O-S-C-A-R, my bologna has a second name, it's M-A-Y-E-R"...and there you have it-jingle, memory, success!

Cereal? Oh, yes, "snap, crackle, pop," I needed Rice Krispies.

Medicine aisle? No problem. Which bandage was it? "I am stuck on Band Aid Brand 'cause Band Aid's stuck on me." What was that medicine I needed last night for my upset stomach? "Plop, plop, fizz, fizz, oh what a relief it is." Of course, thank you jingle. It was Alka-Seltzer I needed.

If I wanted something easy to fix at home, there were no worries because "La Choy makes Chinese food swing American," and I could always pick up Rice-a-Roni, "the San Francisco treat."

Then I could put all the groceries in my car and have enough time to "see the USA in my Chevrolet."

But today's commercials are an absolute emotional mess. They can't just give me a nice simple jingle and call it a day. There is so much emotional baggage that comes with them that it makes me think my friend, the therapist, should put her couch in aisle two of the grocery store and use that as her office address.

Seriously, when I went to the store and tried to remember which beverage to pick up, the last Budweiser Super Bowl commercial came to mind, the one with the puppy and the pony. It took me on such an emotional rollercoaster ride that my husband thought they were playing free Lifetime movies right there in aisle nine. Thank God it had a happy ending or I wouldn't have been able to drive home in one piece.

As for driving today, if they want me to drive a Honda, I have to do it while listening to Bruce Willis talk over soft background piano music about having a hug fest for the safety of my family. By the end of the commercial, I feel that if I don't buy that car, I don't really love my family. It's a whole guilt trip. I can't even finish the trip though because before I go anywhere in my Honda, I have to buy it from CarMax. I have no choice. Rudy Ruettiger will do the slow clap for me, which will make me feel like a hero just for buying a car while listening to a whole symphony.

Some product called Cialis wants me to go back to outdoor plumbing and have an outdoor spa with two separate bathtubs in the middle of a meadow. They've got a whole second honeymoon planned out for me. But if I go to the store and try to remember what product to buy, I have no idea, because all I can think about is a picture of me and my husband naked in the middle of a meadow each with our own separate tubs. Somehow, when I unpack my groceries, two containers of bath salts come out of the bag. Wait, what?

MetLife has a commercial with the Peanuts character, Schroeder, playing the National Anthem on his piano in an empty football stadium. This commercial makes me so patriotic that I have to stand up in my living room with my hand over my heart. I'm not kidding. The dog went and got our American flag out of the closet as a gesture of mutual allegiance.

Extra gum, has a commercial showing a dad making little origami cranes for his daughter on numerous occasions while she's growing up. In the end, the father's loading her car up to ship her off on her own when an entire box of them spills out onto the driveway. All I have to say is it's a good thing I've already sent both by girls off to college and beyond because once I saw that commercial, I never would have been able to do it. That commercial almost made me go into the ugly cry.

I feel sorry for today's youth. I don't know how they're ever going to be able to remember what they need at the store. They'll probably just have to stand in the aisles and have a good cry while sending out a tweet to see if anyone can remember why they came to the store in the first place.

As for me, I can't take it anymore. These commercial adventures are making me rethink my whole life. I may have to stop watching commercials all together. But first, let me go buy some Zoloft and Ambien so I can sleep until my mood swings go away.

To Young People

Every May and June, at the time of graduation ceremonies, I ask myself what I would tell a bunch of wide-eyed kids in their late teens and early twenties about their lives ahead.

People talk about following their passions. If you're in your early twenties, and you've already found your passion, you are fortunate indeed and should follow it. But most of us are not so lucky. We don't know at age twenty, or thirty, or even forty what our mission in life is. We go through life following the motions. We get a job, hopefully in a field we have some interest in. We hope to find someone to love and share our lives with. We decide if we want to share our lives with children. We try to make money, and we try to be a success, whatever that means to us.

Some of these young adults will become doctors, lawyers, politicians. Some will become bankers, stay-at-home parents, ditch diggers, childcare workers, cashiers, or clerks. Some will break the law and end up in jail. Some will become addicts. Some will become sick. Some will not survive to see old age.

So what could I say that might make a difference? I would tell them about three things: kindness, moderation, and passion.

Kindness is a key to me. First it's important to be kind to yourself. It's good to put yourself first as long as you're not the only one on the roster. When you are good to yourself, you are happy, which makes you confident and strong enough to spread kindness to others. When we're older, we often find we have regrets for all kinds of things, but I've never regretted a time when I shared a kindness.

Moderation is good in almost everything. There is nothing wrong with indulging in life's pleasures. Having a few vices is not so terrible. After all, none of us is perfect. But I've always found that moderation brings balance to life. Too much work leads to an unhappy home. Too much play leads to an unsuccessful career. Too much eating makes you fat, unhealthy and uncomfortable in your own skin. Too much dieting makes you mean, unhealthy, and craving the spice of life. Too much people-pleasing prevents pleasing yourself. Too much self-gratification leads to a lonely, unsatisfied life. I believe that living with a dose of everything and an excess of little will serve you well in life.

Now I said that moderation was good in "almost" everything. There is also passion. In my twenties, I didn't think I had a particular passion for anything. I knew that I was good in communications. If I knew how to do something, I was good at teaching others how to do it as well. I knew I was good at public speaking. I never seemed to have a fear of the public, and I knew I was a good listener because I was the one my friends came to in order to be heard. But I didn't feel that I had a burning passion for anything in particular. I remember people telling me that if I followed my passion I would never work a day in my life.

Yet I could pinpoint no passion. When I asked myself what my mission on earth was, I found no answer. So I followed my talents. I worked in fields where I knew I could take advantage of those strengths. I was a "hotelly" which allowed me to use my communications skills to make presentations to clients, book the sale, and listen well to each client's needs. I ran a book fair business that led to continued use of these same talents by writing promotional pieces to advertise upcoming events, listening to customers' wishes, and ordering product that would please them. I worked for a non-profit that encouraged me to speak to large groups and to educate them using my ability to break down large subjects into small chunks. This enabled me to explain a topic in an easy to understand manner. What I didn't know was that I did have passion; I just hadn't found it yet.

I found my first passion when I met my husband. I had the fortune of falling in love. I fell hard, and I fell for life. It didn't always come easily. We had our rough spots, but it was a passion just the same. I've never regretted it. My second passion, which came shortly after the first, was for my children. Most parents I know feel the same, but my passion was to be a stay-at-home mom, even though it was very unfashionable to do so at the time. The prior generation of women had fought long and hard for the right to build careers and be super-women. They fought so that we could be wives, mothers, and have careers. I was out of step, but I followed my passion against my friends' paths into medicine, law and finance. I've never regretted my decision.

But eventually, if we've done a good job, our children grow up and move on with their own lives, to follow their own dreams. It wasn't until this later period in my life that I found my other passion: writing. If I'm pissed off at the world for attempting to take away the civil rights of a fellow human being, I can write about it. If I'm touched by the kindness I observe in someone, I can write about it. If my mind won't stop racing because it has so much it wants to share, I can write about it.

When I start writing, it takes my full bladder or my growling stomach to tell me to step away from the keyboard and practice moderation.

What do I think is important for today's youth to know? My answer is to practice kindness, moderation, and passion in life. Whatever your choices are, if you practice these three things, your regrets will be small and your successes will not only be abundant, but they will come from your heart.

A Final Note

Each night, when I lay my head against my pillow, next to my best friend, I reach over to turn out the light on my nightstand. When I do, I glance down at my most prized material possession: a thirty-eight-year-old hockey puck my husband caught for me on our first date. Every night, it makes me smile, and every night, I am grateful.

Thank you for allowing me to share my stories with you. I know that you've had challenges in your life too. I hope you know you're not alone. I've always felt that it's ok to acknowledge the rough patches. It's ok to call in for support when you find yourself empty. To me, the key is to be able to get back up and try to put it all into perspective. The exclamations of "oh rats" in my children's childhood game taught me as much as it taught them. It taught me that stuff is gonna happen whether we like it or not. Financial crises come and go, 9/11 came and went, cancer came, and came, and came, and will be back, but it's all ok. I'm here to honestly say I wouldn't be the person I am without those things having happened in my life. When people say that money can't buy you happiness, I understand what they mean. While winning the lottery would certainly make me happier, it alone could never bring me happiness. I had to experience a little suffering along the way to be able to appreciate the joys of life. Because it's the little problems like mice, age related memory loss, and screaming birds that made me acknowledge there are much bigger problems in the world that I have faced and overcome, there are considerably bigger problems in the world that I've never had to face, and that the abundance of love I have in my life makes me the kind of wealthy you just can't take to the bank.

Acknowledgements

Thank you mostly to my family for supporting me in this crazy idea of writing. Thank you Nicole and Samantha for helping me with the tedious task of editing.

Thank you Donna Cavanagh of HO-Shorehouse Books for believing enough in me to publish this book.

Thank you Eric Walter of WHYY for publishing my first story and allowing me to believe I could write.

Thank you to the following publications for previously publishing some of the essays in this book and for continuing to publish my work:

WHYY

The Philadelphia Inquirer

HuffPost

Senior Wire News Service

HumorOutcasts

BoomerCafe

ZestNow

If you enjoyed this book, please take a moment to post a review on Amazon. You'll feel good that you did something kind, and both our glasses will be filled.

    -- Thanks Leslie

10736743R00096

Made in the USA
Lexington, KY
30 September 2018